MAN OF AMMAN:
THE LIFE OF DAI DAVIES

D1823679

Man of Amman:
The Life of Dai Davies

Phil Melling

First Impression—March 1994

© Phil Melling

ISBN 1 85902 083 6

Printed in Wales
at the Gomer Press, Llandysul, Dyfed

For
Sean and Tim
in Coomastow, County Kerry

Contents

Acknowledgements

I would never have met Dai Davies if I hadn't sat in Dai Hughes's seat in the bar of The Rhyddings. It was 1978 and I had recently arrived in Brynmill, Swansea from the north of England. I was renting a flat not a hundred yards from the Swansea Rugby ground and feeling acutely disoriented. They called the ground St. Helen's, but this wasn't Knowsley Road and no one knew, or if they did I never heard them say, who 'the Saints' were or what happened on Good Friday, and even though Roy Mathias came from Llanelli no one mentioned his name on match days. At two thirty everyone shouted 'Come on the Whites' and clapped politely whenever the stand-off, who was flashy and apparently had A levels and couldn't tackle for toffee, hoofed it into touch. Not surprisingly, I was in a state of deep shock. I was also paranoid for I knew I had to be careful of the things I said in public in case of reprisal from those on the lookout for spies and scouts. I kept quiet as best I could but I couldn't keep quiet all the time and I was hungry for gossip—stories of Rugby League players who had 'gone north', how many and when.

As it turned out, I needn't have worried. There were plenty of people like Dai Hughes in The Rhyddings who were more than ready to name some names and talk about the old days without fear of reprisal. Dai it was who took me on a journey I shall never forget one wet, foggy, November night, a night so awful it had, for a Wiganer, words like Post Office Road and Odsal Stadium written all over it. We drove to Garnant through Clydach, Pontardawe and Gwauncaegurwen. It was a road into folklore. Dai told stories all the way

up. The stories were good but they made me nervous. I didn't know what I'd find at the end of them and I didn't even know if the people Dai talked of wanted to be found. Paranoia was an easy affliction in those days. 'Apocalypse, Now' had just come out and I felt like Willard going back up the Mekong with Dai as the guide. We were headed due north, Dai said, to the Garnant Constitutional Club. There was a good chance we'd run into the guru of Garnant, the living legend of Rugby League, Ted Ward himself. Ted was in his sixties and had a touch of shingles but still enjoyed his bottle of Gold Label. On a wet, Thursday night Ted would be sitting at a table by the door.

I had spent the afternoon with a Rugby League Yearbook getting the facts right. I also dug out a folder with photos and clippings of newspaper articles written by the late Eric Thompson about a memory-lane trip he had taken in the sixties through the valleys of South Wales. I also had a souvenir brochure issued by Wigan the week after Jim Sullivan died. Jim had been Ted Ward's coach and the brochure contained two of the most moving obituaries I had ever read, one from Cliff Webb, the other from Vince Karalius.

I met Ted Ward. He was sitting by the door, as Dai had said. We talked a lot about Wigan and I showed him the photographs of the team he played for in the 1940s, the ones in the brochure with Joe Egan, Ken Gee, Cec Mountford and Tommy Bradshaw. I also showed him what the journalists and players said about Jim Sullivan. After a while Ted grew silent, we shifted tables and I found myself in more animated company. I was immediately confronted by a wild-eyed imp in a Warrington Rugby League Club blazer shouting an order to a friend at the bar. The blazer came close. It told me to take no notice of Ted. 'Ted Ward knows nothing', it said. 'Talk to me. I know it all'.

And it did. For the next twelve years Dai Davies was all talk. He never shut up. Whoever he was he was certainly no Kurtz. He was irresistible and wherever he is now and whatever defence he happens to be tormenting, a word of thanks to Dai for never saying no when I asked for an interview. Thanks also to his lovely wife Kate for looking after me on my visits to Garnant and the hospitality she showed me. Some people you feel you've always known and Kate was one of them, a warm, generous and elegant lady.

I couldn't have written this book without the help of Dai's son, Bill Davies, and I thank him for the journeys he made on my behalf and the hours he spent pouring over copies of the *Amman Valley Chronicle* in Carmarthen Library. I must also thank him for the loan of the family albums and photographs and the occasional interview he did with Dai on my behalf.

I would also like to acknowledge the work of John Burn in Manchester whose love affair with Broughton Rangers remains strong after all these years. John went to a great effort in visiting the libraries of Greater Manchester at his own expense. The material he uncovered on Dai's career in national and local newspapers was simply invaluable.

Ernie Day also supplied me with information on Dai's career at Warrington. I thank him for his proof reading of the manuscript and the contacts he gave me at Warrington Museum. Alan Leigh, Director of the Museum, was courteous and helpful whenever I requested information on archival material. Robert Gate was his usual, meticulous self whenever I asked for help in proof reading. Robert is a one-off, unrivalled as an historian and statistician of Rugby League. Mick Rhodes assisted (as he does so many people) when I urgently needed photographs of Dai at Huddersfield. Eurof Walters of Amman was also generous in loaning me rare illustrations and in providing me with information on Dai's early career with Amman United. David Evans of Brynaman kindly loaned me a number of the photographs he had taken and collected over the years.

The following individuals and organisations were helpful and I wish to record my thanks to them. J. M. Holliday, Bill Shankland, Hywel Teifi Edwards, Kevin Thomas, Peter Stead, Clive Griffiths, Raymond Fletcher, Jon Roper, Roger Davies (Arts photographer, University College Swansea), Peter Northcott, Jack McNamara, Tim Auty, Anne Marshall, Jack Hamblett, Peter Corcoran, Sharon Hansard, Neath Rugby Football Club, Keighley Rugby League Supporters club, and, most of all, Susan Melling.

Preface

Whenever Dai Davies was asked who was the best player to come out of Wales, his eyes would light up and he would say he was. He was half-joking, certainly, but he was also half-serious. He had tremendous ability and he knew it and that is often the sign of a great player. Dai made his name as a scrum-half with Amman United and Neath before being lured north to Manchester by Broughton Rangers in the 1925-26 season. The following season his brother Jack, captain and full-back of Ammanford, also went north to Keighley, eventually moving on to Dewsbury for whom he dropped a goal in the first Rugby League Cup final at Wembley when Wigan beat his team 13-2.

If Jack Davies thought that was bad luck, it was small beer when set beside brother Dai's Wembley experiences. Dai had the unprecedented bad fortune to play for three different clubs at Wembley and finished on the losing team on each occasion. After struggling along with Broughton Rangers for a couple of years Dai was transferred in 1927 to Warrington with whom he spent the seven best years of his career. Within five months of arriving at Wilderspool he was on Warrington's wing for the last pre-Wembley Challenge Cup Final which saw Swinton beat the Wires 5-3 at Wigan in 1928. In 1932-33 Dai scored a try in the Lancashire Cup Final as Warrington beat St. Helens 10-9 at Wigan. On the same ground later in the season Davies scored perhaps the most crucial try of his Warrington career in the third round of the Challenge Cup. Late in the match Wigan led 7-4 when a scrum went down and Dai produced his party trick, an electrifying short burst from the scrum base down the blind-side to score at the corner flag without a Wigan hand laid on him. Fullback Billy Holding had to clear a way between piles of straw and milling ringside spectators but landed a miraculous goal to send Warrington on the road to Wembley for the first time.

The 1933 Wembley final was a classic. Davies played a blinder, scoring two characteristic tries straight from scrums but Huddersfield pipped the Wires 21-17. Oddly enough, although several players have since emulated Dai's tally of two tries in Wembley Finals, no one has yet beaten it.

In 1935 Dai Davies was transferred to Huddersfield and appeared in his second Wembley Final within three months of signing. Five of the Fartown backs were Welsh including his stand-off partner Gwyn Richards. Again it was a close run affair but Huddersfield went down 11-8 to Castleford. Dai's final move was to Keighley in 1936 where he was made captain. In 1937 his team astonished the Rugby League fraternity by reaching Wembley for the only time in the club's history. This time there were eight Welshmen in Dai's team but again he was to receive only a loser's medal as Widnes won 18-5. The game was in fact the last Dai played. He had played 335 first-class matches in an eleven-year career. Although he made a habit of losing at Wembley—he lost whilst playing for Wales against Australia there in 1930 and 1933 in addition to three losing Cup Finals—his real worth is reflected in four caps for Wales, one for the Other Nationalities and five for Glamorgan & Monmouthshire. In 1932 he played two tour trials and was regarded as most unfortunate to miss tour selection.

In his prime at Warrington he was a match-winner, blessed with astonishing speed over the first 10-15 yards and a master craftsman around the scrum-base. His short half-back partnership with fellow Welshman Tommy Flynn (ex-Tal-y-waun) bears comparison with any half-back pairing to have played for the club. Dai was tall for a scrum-half but looked frail and he was not a great tackler but his speed off the mark and marvellous artistry with the ball in his hands more than made up for any defensive defects. He was unquestionably one of the great halfbacks of his era.

ROBERT GATE

1: Where I Lived

I was born in Caenewydd, Gwauncaegurwen, same place as Gareth Edwards, and I remember when I was about four and a half to five years of age my father and mother had gone to Swansea and bought me a rugby ball. Whether that started my career as a footballer I do not know but they also bought me a pair of hobnail boots. I was so thrilled with the boots I wore them in bed that night. First thing in the morning I went down with my other brothers—they were older than me, of course—to play in a field that we called 'the cwt', and there I started kicking my first rugby ball.

Later I went to school on the Waun, and I remember that those living in Caenewydd, they had to go to Tai'r-gwaith school. I remember when it opened because I shoved my hand in one of the closet doors in the yard. Somebody slapped it and off went the skin on

two or three fingers and I was sent home bandaged up.

In the meantime, my father and my eldest brother, Tom, the one who was killed in the First World War, they started work in the Gelli Ceidrim Colliery. They tried to get a house for us down there and eventually we went down and lived in the house that was built by where Les James lives now, in Glanaman. We lived there for a few years and then we moved to Ceidrim Terrace on the main road, number 3, where Byron Phillips lives. We lived there for quite a while and then we had to move again, 'flit', as they say in Lancashire, this time to a damp house. As soon as the council school opened in Garnant we had to move from Glanaman school. I was in Standard 6 when the new school opened and my first teacher was Edryd Jones, the *pregethwr* from Bethel. I left after Standard 7

Caenewydd, Gwauncaegurwen, where Dai was born. This photograph, taken in the 1920s, shows the building of the Welfare Hall on the left.

and I started work in the Gelli Ceidrim Colliery. I was fourteen years of age.

I should like to mention a few incidents regarding the time I was at school in Garnant.

I remember once going home to have dinner, me and a boy named Mal Jones[1]—he turned out to be a hairdresser, dead and buried now. We went up to Pistyll Llwyd farm and we were up to our eyeballs in clay and late coming back. It was about quarter past two and the teacher saw us, Mr. Williams from Llanelli. I didn't like him at all; he was a tyrant in my estimation. Anyway, we went into the classroom to join our pals—Percy Rees and Dai John Thomas—and we thought we would sneak into our seats. Unfortunately, Williams saw us. 'Where are you going back there?' he shouted. And he told us to stand in front of the class. As it happened Mal was standing in front of me and Williams said, 'Look at your feet, Jones. Look at the mess on your boots'. Mal put his head down and as he did Williams let fly with a flathander and hit Mal clean off his pegs. Mal gave such a scream, got up and ran to his seat. 'Course it was your friend Davey next and there I was standing in front. I was a much smaller boy than Mal and Williams said to me—but I kept my eyes on him, I never took my eyes off him—'Look at your feet, Davies'. I still kept looking at him and Williams let fly. But Davey wasn't there. No, sir. He ducked underneath and slap-happy Williams went headlong on the floor. I took to my heels, opened the door and ran right into the hands of the headmaster, Mr. Edwards, who took me to his room. Williams told him what I had done, showed him my boots and, of course, he made sure I had four on each hand. But I took it. I would rather the stick than what Mal Jones had.

Dai Davies, upper right, with members of his family in 1912. Lower right is Dai's brother, Moss, who lived most of his life in Hammersmith before settling in Paisley with his wife and son. Dai's sister, Deveene, lower left, died of a virus in 1955 after serving as a nurse in Burma during the Second World War. Dai's mother, Anne, upper left, was a gentle and expansive woman, the rock of the family. She died in August 1925, aged fifty seven. Dai's elder sister, Lizzie Anne, is standing centre.

Garnant and Glanaman with Ceidrim Terrace bottom left. Dai's house is second from the left.

After Ceidrim Terrace Dai's family moved to 6, Evans Terrace, extreme left, in the row to the right. This particular photograph, taken in the 1940s, shows the old Gelli Ceidrim Colliery buildings at the bottom. In the centre of the photograph is Bethel Chapel where Dai was dragged as a child. Top left is the Amman United Ground. A game or training is taking place.

Garnant School.

This dairy may well have taken milk from Pistyll Llwyd farm.

A marvellous photograph of a Garnant ironmonger's shop around the turn of the century.

There were quite a number of incidents during my time in school. I was once in the girl's yard, along with my pal Percy Rees, and he took short. Percy said: 'I'm going to the toilet'. So I said: 'You go on then'. Little did we know that you could see into the toilets, boys and girls, from the school classroom. Old Edwards, the headmaster— Gooseberry Whiskers we called him—must have seen us. He came down into the toilets and gave me a clout behind the ear. I ran into the yard followed by Percy with his trousers hanging down. Edwards gave him a slap on the butt and Percy turned round. 'You bloody old Gooseberry Whiskers', he said.

Just before I left school some of the lads went on strike. Dai Madge was our leader and the teachers were frightened to death of him. Dai and the lads were walking through the classes and I remember they came into

our class and we joined them. After that we walked into the yard and there we were marching and playing football and the teachers like Williams and old Gooseberry Whiskers couldn't do a thing. We hated a lot of our teachers. I remember the day Williams was called up for the army. They came round and asked us would we like to give something towards a present before he went off. He'd given us such a hammering from time to time and in any case, we couldn't afford it. I'd got my father and two brothers in the army and things for me were very bad at home. There was only Jack who was working. All the other lads brought something, 3d, 4d or 6d, but me and Moss didn't bring a thing. We were in bad books with the teacher, the one who was organising the collection, and she talked about us to the class. I hated that woman. She was a woman who cycled all the way from

Pontardawe. I was hoping she'd have a puncture and have to walk it. There were plenty like her when I was at school.

One day my brother Moss and me—he was in Standard 6 and I was in Standard 7—we were standing in line in the school yard. The teacher we had was a nasty thing. Jenny Vaughan her name was. Moss and I were pushing in the line and old Vaughan had a pointer in her hand and a bell. All of a sudden she hit me with the bell and caught me over the mouth and I was bleeding bad. Moss started imitating her so she hit out and caught him as well and he started bleeding. Moss and me saw red and we started kicking her and belting her. She ran into the school and out came old Gooseberry Whiskers. He brought us in and slapped us. But the few kicks we gave her, believe you me, it was worth every belt.

Jenny Vaughan lived next door to us in Glanaman. In each house the toilet was at the top of the garden. The evening after the incident the Vaughan woman came out of her house to go to the toilet. My father followed her. He'd been washing up and had a dinner plate in his hand and he challenged her about this incident with my brother and me. As he spoke Jenny Vaughan turned round and gave him some backchat. My father got annoyed and held the plate up in the air. 'You'd better go up to that toilet of yours as fast as your legs can carry you, Miss Vaughan' he said, 'Otherwise, I'll crack this plate over your blooming bottom'.

I left school at fourteen and went into the Gelli Ceidrim colliery. The under manager was James Enoch James. I started off on the screens and got moved to the belts picking slag. I was then shunted to the cobbles and from there I went underground. I started working as a door-boy with a haulier called Tom Lewis. Every Friday on payday the

Gelli Ceidrim Colliery.

hauliers used to give something to the door-boy but this fella of mine, Tom Lewis, he was such a skinflint I got nothing and the other boys had half a crown each. I suppose Tom wasn't all mean. When he killed a pig he used to bring in a lump of boiled meat. I couldn't eat the meat but my dad enjoyed it.

After a few years I got pulled out. I was unemployed and doing nothing for quite a while. When I started back I was with a fella called Rees Owen in the big vein. Door-boy again. Then I went on to the faces. I was with a rider, pulling wires. I was not a big fella and I could hardly lift the knocker up. Rees was pretty good as a physical fellow. He played football with the local team as a hooker. I remember him telling me how he became so physically fit. He said it was all down to deep breathing and told me to do some shadow boxing to develop my chest. He was right. I couldn't get into the local team because I was small. So I persevered with what Rees told me and eventually I put a bit of weight on.

I left Rees Owen as door-boy and became assistant repairer with my dad. I had a good time with my father because he never let me work hard. The thing I was most frightened of underground were the old workings in the mines. Some chaps knew where the workings were, like my dad—he knew the old workings —but I didn't. I remember one day, on the afternoon shift, they started shouting and telling us to get out. 'All out', they yelled. 'Get out'. But I'd lost my father. He knew where to go—one of the old airways—but I didn't. I began walking with another chap from the big vein. The water was rushing out of the old workings and the gas came with it. Our oil lamps were dead and this chap, Gwyn Banwen, got hold of my coat and we walked our way up to Number 2 face. My ears were bunged up and I couldn't hear a thing.

Afterwards, when I got up top I had a bath and went to the surgery. Doctor Rees syringed my ears and the stuff that came out you wouldn't believe. I was alright then. We'd come up through the gas, of course. Lucky for us our lamps had gone out. We'd have been blown to bits if Gwyn or me had been holding a lamp and it had been lit.

There was a dispute in the Gelli colliery and for a while I worked a spell in the Llanharan colliery with my brother Jack. We got on well together. We were a close family. My youngest sister was twelve and there was the eldest sister and of my brothers at home

Gelli Ceidrim Colliery officials in the 1920s. Dai would have known and possibly worked with these men.

Dai's father, David Rees Davies (Dai 'Cender' Sr.), upper right. He is pictured at Ffair-fach old people's home, Llandeilo, in the early 1950s. According to Dai, 'the old man' was a hard worker and a strict disciplinarian well known for his love of the booze and the Bible.

there was only Moss left. The youngest sister was going to grammar school and that was in Ammanford and she was very attached to my eldest sister and she was going down to visit her all the time. Will had gone to America. There wasn't much of the family left and later on my father decided to break up the home. It damn near killed me when that happened, you know. It was bad enough to lose my mother. Mother and I were great pals.

I remember before she died my father had pleurisy. I'd gone to bed one morning and was working nights. She called out to me to make a poultice for her. 'A mustard and linseed poultice', she shouted. I was half asleep when I got up and I shouted to my dad, 'Get your shirt up, dad, and I'll bring you the

poultice'. I put this lump of mustard on the linseed poultice and when I slapped it on him he gave such a shout. '*Beth ddiawl wyt ti wedi 'neud?*' (What the devil have you done?) Later on when they took the poultice off they found it had stripped the skin off him. But I'll tell you this. It cured him of pleurisy. I don't think any doctor could have made a better poultice.

My father was a hell of a lad. One Friday night he was in bed while the rest of us were having supper. One of my brothers said: 'What's the matter with him tonight? He's supposed to be going out?' Father had had a few in the afternoon, see, and he'd overslept. We soon heard his foot getting out of the bed but he'd gone to bed with his socks on and in the dark he stepped on the mat at the top of the stairs. The next thing was we could hear his legs go up in the air. Down he came on his bottom. Never missed a blooming step on the stairs—bump, bump, bump. Down he came and into the passage 'til there he was sprawled on the mat. My brother Jack said: 'By damn, the old fella's in a hurry tonight!' There he was flat on his back and there we were acting the goat and falling about. Dad looked up and said: '*Damo chi. Beth ddiawl, 'newch rywbeth nage disgwl!*' (Damn you. Do something besides looking!)

I had two sisters. Lizzie Ann was older than me and she married Elwyn Davies from Ammanford, a nice, quiet chap who died in his fifties. Deveene was younger. She died of a virus when she was in her forties. I also had five brothers—six, counting the first-born, Rees, who died as a baby.[2] Glyn, the youngest brother, died as a young boy. He had to have a leg amputated after an injury with a cork ball on a day he was playing cricket. Things happened like that in those days. Tom was killed in the First World War in 1918. He was my eldest brother and a fine fella. Chapel going, different than any of the other brothers, you know. My father was in the war as well. He was in the Lancashires and was fifty years of age at the time. One of my brothers, Moses—our Moss—he went to London and finished up in Paisley. We used to correspond. He told me once his son worked in a bank and asked me to visit him, but I never went up there.

My other brother, Will, the one that went abroad, he was in the Merchant Navy and then he was in America.[3] Will travelled all over the world. He was fifteen years in America and he went to every state in the Union. Oh, he could name them all. He even went to Alaska. That's where he met the actor. What's his name, the one with the

Dai's eldest brother, Tom, was killed on the Somme. It came as a great shock to the family when they learned by telegram that Tom was 'missing presumed dead'. In the 1970s Nev Anthony of Garnant found Tom's name on a memorial at the Pozière war cemetery.

moustache? He's dead and buried now. Clark Gable—that's it. He worked in Alaska as a logger. That's where Will met him. They picked him up and made an actor out of him. Then there was Dempsey, world heavyweight champion, professional. He died not so long ago. He fought Tunney. He was a lumberjack as well. They were all for fighting and drinking —beer or whisky, Will said—and Dempsey could slosh any of them. Some scout picked him up. They saw his prospects and they made a heavyweight boxer out of him. Will knew Dempsey. He went in his restaurant.

Dai's brother, Will, was barely sixteen when he enlisted in the cavalry in the First World War.

I remember we slapped one of them—Harry Slocombe—and he ran like a hare to the house, frightened. There were riots in Ammanford and a few got caught. They were charged and brought to trial at Carmarthen Assizes. I remember I went to the court. It was the first time I ever saw a fella with a wig on. The prisoners were brought up from below in chains. There was Jack and Harry '*Bach*' Jones and Phil Isaac and Freddy James. They were only pickets but they each got a fortnight in Swansea jail.[4] It was a terrible sentence. A pal of my brother Jack, Hopkin Jones, he had a big bag of fruit with him and he shouted out: 'Don't worry, lads, you won't starve!' And, by damn, they didn't. Two busloads of us went down to meet them the day they were released.

Dempsey had a big restaurant in New York and my brother went in there. He didn't see Dempsey—someone said Dempsey was away on business—but he heard the music, a blooming, big organ in Dempsey's restaurant. Huge place, Will said.

There wasn't much for you if you stayed at home. In 1925 we had a strike in the mines for three months and in the summer we were picketing them in the colliery. My brother Jack wasn't involved at all in the picketing but he happened to be on the committee of the Lodge at the Gelli Ceidrim Colliery. There was one particular evening we were picketing and we stopped a few of the officials.

Will, seated extreme left, riding the rails in the 1920s. 'Boxcar Willy' was the lovable rogue of the family, a hobo who fell in love with long distance in his teens. At the time this photograph was taken Will had just finished a stint as a grave-digger during the great flu epidemic that swept America in the mid 1920s. Will died of lung cancer in 1972.

The anthracite strikers, some of whom were jailed in 1926. Bottom left are Phil Isaacs and Percy Rees. Rees (third from left, sitting) was Dai's half-back partner at the Amman United. He died of pneumonia in the 1950s.

Singing and dancing up the street we were and we gave them a reception and bought a big meal. I didn't drink much. Lemonade perhaps. We went home in the bus.

During the strike there was a colliery in Crynant and some of the miners in Crynant carried on working. We had a meeting on the Cwmaman Park and they came from Ammanford and Brynaman—everywhere in the Aman Valley. We passed a vote and decided we'd march to Crynant and land there just before the day shift came on. Hundreds of us went. We marched with an escort over the mountain and we were just like an army, a big army ready to charge from the top of the height. Then we came down off the mountain and waited. Some of the boys went along to the colliery but we stayed put at

the railway station for the colliers from Neath. When the trains landed the colliers got out and ran like hell down the line and we threw sods at them. There was a cop. You could tell he was scared. Later at the colliery someone threw a sod and caught the cop in the head. He turned all colours. One of the colliery officials got slapped a few times. We frightened off the colliers and stopped the mine. Then we went back to Neath on the train.

Sometime after 1925 my mother died and my father split the home up. My youngest sister went to live in Ammanford. I have a lot of memories of Ammanford. Believe it or not there were people in Ammanford who'd come from Wigan: the Gerrards and Hewletts and Darbyshires. They'd come to work in

Ammanford at the Betws Colliery, and Mr. Hewlett was the manager and lived in Ammanford. These people came down to show the Welsh people, the Welsh miners, how to dig coal. They found their mistake soon enough. What we had there was a different type of coal to what they were used to. This was anthracite coal and they thought they could hole it when you had to bore it and shoot it. But never mind, they were a grand lot of fellows, whatever their foolishness.

I knew them well. Especially Jim Darbyshire. He was the under manager and he was rugby mad. My brother Jack was well away with him. He always used to be with Jim Darbyshire after a game of rugby. Jack played fullback for Ammanford and he was in the first cup final at Wembley Stadium in 1929. He kicked the first goal there.[5] That was funny him being with the Dewsbury club and playing against Wigan and his pal back in Ammanford coming from Wigan. Jack was very pally with Jim Darbyshire. Jim often stayed here in our house. He opened a bookmaker's shop in Ammanford. He was always a good hearted fella. Threw money about like anything... very generous. That's all I can say about people from Wigan, Jim Darbyshire especially. Course he's dead and gone now, like a lot of them.[6]

NOTES

[1] The *Amman Valley Chronicle,* 10 January 1925 has a report of the Amman v Resolven game in which Dai Davies is partnered by Mal Jones at half back.

[2] Dai is unusually modest about the sporting talents of his family. In 1923 the *Amman Valley Chronicle* makes the following observation. 'Mr. David Davies of 6, Evans Terrace, Glanamman can be justly proud of his sons' capabilities as footballers—David Morgan who operates at inside half for the Amman; Jack, Ammanford's custodian; and Moses who plays at inside half for Amman Seconds. William, another son, who is at present in America, was one of the Amman's stalwarts and a forward of merit. To revert to David Morgan Davies, he partners Percy Rees as a scrum worker. As a pair those two are the youngest playing in Wales in class football. On the visit of Llanelli to Glanaman, Davies proved himself brilliant and I say it without fear of contradiction that on the day's form he easily outshone the Scarlets experienced scrum worker. Again on Saturday at Skewen, he gave a repetition of his cleverness and proved that apart from his lack of weight, he is equal to any half in the Principality. Should he be able to keep free for a few seasons from being abused by heavy opposition, I can predict nothing less than International honours for him'.

'Cwmamman Football Brothers', Cwmamman Topics, 'Tee Tan', *Amman Valley Chronicle,* 20 September 1923.

[3] Will lied about his age and fought in World War I when he was fifteen and a half. In 1981 during an exhibition of Rugby League photographs and souvenirs commemorating the achievements of Welsh players, I brought Dai to my house, an old property which had previously been split into flats. Dai claimed to remember the house and that either this or the one next door had been rented by Will in the last years of his life. He took me upstairs and showed me Will's room, a third floor attic. Dai's son, Bill Davies, also confirmed that Will came to the end of his travels in Finsbury Terrace, Brynmill.

[4] Dai's story is corroborated and a fuller account of the trial is provided in an article entitled 'The Gelli Ceidrim Raid, Assizes Proceedings', *Amman Valley Chronicle,* 10 December 1925.

[5] Jim Sullivan of Wigan kicked the first goal at Wembley. Jack Davies did, however, kick the first drop goal. Wigan beat Dewsbury 13-2.

[6] Jim Derbyshire was also councillor in Ammanford and Chairman of Ammanford Rugby Club in the immediate pre-war era.

2: What I Lived For

I've said I remember my dad and mother going to Swansea. I'd say I was about four years of age, you know, and they bought me a football. The old man must have had an instinct that I was going to be a sweet shot. I was football mad. There was no television or nothing like that in those days. Families were big then, not one or two. Some of them were even eleven or twelve. Today, they've got to look for players to make up the team but in those days, when I was young, you would blow the whistle and there would be an avalanche of football players.

We played with a tin, any dashed thing. If someone killed a pig there was always a bladder. We'd ask for it and play with it. We played on the road and on the tips ... all of us like blacks grabbing hold of one another. I don't know how I survived because I was so small. But isn't it funny? Out of all those my age, I was the only one that made the grade. I was the only one that really got on. I played here in Garnant school and we were pretty good. We had to play on the football ground, the Amman United Ground. You can see it from here, from the house. We called it the park.

One day we had a date with the county school and they were booked to play us up here. That meant a few hours off from lessons. The master picking the team, Edwards his name was, came from a place called Llandeilo. He came here when the school opened. Everybody thought I'd be in the team. But I wasn't in the team. Edwards never picked me. I was so small, you know. When he didn't pick me, *Duw,* I took black. I was very upset. This teacher insulted me. I don't

remember what happened to the school and whether they won their game or not. After he'd ignored me I wasn't interested in the result. To think that I was not considered big enough and yet I went on to play for Amman United.

When I went to the Amman there was a fella there called Joe Griffiths—he died about six months back in Clydach—and he was a lot older than me. He had been picked for Llanelli when the scrum half at Llanelli—Arthur John he was called—got injured. When Joe went they asked me to turn out for Amman United. At the time I was playing for the second team, Amman Rangers, the A team as they say in Lancashire. I agreed to play in the first team and after that Joe Griffiths never got his place back. You understand? He came back from Llanelli and he had to play for Amman United—in the seconds.

All our family played football—bar the eldest, the one that was killed in the war. Jack was third eldest and went to Keighley, then he was transferred to Dewsbury. He couldn't get his place here in Amman United's team, so he went to Ammanford. Jack was older than me. He was about three years older. He went north in 1927. My idol at Amman United was the fullback, Joe Rees, Billo Rees' brother. Joe Plough they called him—on account of him living near the Plough and Harrow. Joe was a great fullback. He fought in the First World War, then he came back home and played for Swansea. I was only ten when I first saw him. Later on he worked in the same colliery as me. Joe's brother, Billo Rees, played for Swinton in that great side of

Joe Rees of Amman and Swansea. Dai said that, with the exception of Jim Sullivan, Joe Rees was the best full back he ever saw.

theirs. They were a family of footballers, the Reeses. You could pick a team from among their relations.

Before I started playing we went down to Amman United and watched the team kick goals. We used to field the ball at practice and kick it back to them. I lived on the park. Nowadays you can't whip them down there. Today, the place is empty. As kids we used to pick sides. I used to swank passing a ball. You'd watch a player, your idol you know, or somebody like him. And you picked things up. Better than having lessons or sums. I'd say to my friends, 'No school today, lads. It's classes on the park'. And down I'd go and watch the players. I'd go and watch whoever was practising and if I liked the look of him I'd do the same—whoever he was.

When we picked sides as kids we didn't play the whole length of the Amman United pitch, just crossways see. We had two captains. You can bet whoever won the toss I was first choice. Later on, after we left school, we had a team called Prospect Stars and we never got beaten. My stand off was a fella called Percy Rees. He died later of pneumoconiosis. Someone has a picture of that team and I was in it and Percy Rees was in it. On the wing was Wally Watkins. He had a trial with Broughton through me. Then there was

Sammy Evans and Myrddin Jones and Dai Rees and his brother, Tom. Tom was a wing, pretty good too, but he didn't go any further. The rest of them stuck with Amman United and then they faded and finished.

Our headquarters was The Half Moon. It was also the dressing rooms. I remember the first game I played for Amman United. It was against a team called Tumble and I was sitting down outside The Half Moon with the lads from The Prospect Stars and I remember the Sec. of Amman United coming up to the team. 'Pick Dai', said the lads. 'Oh he's too small', said the Sec. But the lads went on at him. Eventually I did get picked and I played in the team. I don't say I played a special game, nothing like that you know, but I did O.K. I was only a youngster then, about sixteen or seventeen.

At Amman I played with Jack Elwyn Evans. He had one cap against Scotland, 1924, at Inverleith. Him and me went north to Broughton. Jack was a wing and quite a lot older. He was in the First World War while I was in school. After Amman United he played for Llanelli. I played against him when I signed for Neath. Then there was Evan Phillips. He lived below us. He went to Broughton but not for long.

They were all older than me, see. Same with Rees Owen, the hooker. Billo Rees and Billo Rees' cousin, Joseph Henry—he played for Llanelli now and again. Then there was Billo's brother, Rees Rees. Rees was a centre. He went to Hull K.R. but didn't do much. The Reeses had seven lads—Nathan, Dai, Charles, Joe, Glyn, Rees and Billo.

Billo was the one who made it big. Some said he was selfish and never went out of his way to help the chaps who went north. But it wasn't all roses for Billo, you know. When he went to Swinton he couldn't get his place. A fella named Bert Jenkins from Pen-y-graig in

14

Amman United 2nd XV, 1922-23. Top Row: F. W. Gunning (Chairman), W. Thomas (Committee), M. J. Evans, Jack Evans, C. Lloyd, B. Davies, L. Jones, S. Davies, M. Jones (Trainer), J. Bowen (Committee), D. Morgan (Committee). Middle Row: J. Jones (Trainer), W. Goss, T. Rees, S. Evans, I. Lloyd (Captain), D. Richards, E. Evans, D. Williams, W. Williams. Sitting: P. Rees, D. M. Davies.

Amman United R.F.C. 1922-23. Top Row: B. Jones (Committee), D. Evans (Committee), E. Rees (Committee), I. Rees (Committee), F. W. Gunning (Chairman), E. Jones (Committee), N. Rees, E. Davies, E. Phillips, F. Griffiths, E. Rogers, G. Griffiths, F. Phillips (Referee), W. A. Hay (Secretary), J. Williams (Committee), M. C. Williams (Committee), D. B. Evans. Middle Row: D. J. Jones, R. M. Lewis (Trainer), E. Fowler, S. Evans, T. Evans (Captain), R. Davies, E. Hughes, E. W. Thomas (Secretary), J. H. Griffiths. Front Row: L. Jones, D. Thomas, P. Rees, D. M. Davies.

Billo Rees, tough and lightning-quick. According to Robert Gate, Billo was 'the most celebrated Welsh stand off of the 1920s'. Billo came from Garnant, played for Llanelli and was signed by Swinton in 1921.

the Rhondda was first team stand off. Billo came back to Glanaman for a year and worked in the mines rather than play in the A team at Swinton. I remember he bought a brand new Norton with his signing on fee and we were there on the stones facing the traffic outside The Half Moon. Billo came roaring up and tried to turn round in top gear but he hit the wall of the pub and buckled the front wheel. Billo didn't care. He said he didn't anyway. When Bert Jenkins packed in Billo went back. Billo was a good player—a very good player—but he didn't mix well. Always looked after himself, liked to hear himself praised. I preferred Billo's brother, Joe Rees. Joe had twelve caps for Wales. They say he had a trial with Swinton and wasn't good enough. Whether that was true or not, I don't know. Joe was certainly a hard bugger. Never liked being beaten, especially with a sidestep. Not that Joe was beaten all that often. In my opinion he was the best of the Reeses.

I was at Amman United when Billo went north. I was working nights in the pit with my father—assistant repairer—and the war was on. We were drafted afternoons and that prevented me from training with the boys. The secretary of Amman United, Will Hay,

said if I wanted to play I'd have to work days, so they gave me a job working days. When I started off I was playing for Amman Seconds, but I was soon into the Firsts.

I left my dad and went working on the coal with my brother Jack. Good wages. My brother wouldn't work for nothing. He was a beggar for fighting for a decent wage.

I wasn't with the Amman for long. And then I started playing with Neath. A pal of mine, Garfield Phillips, mentioned my name to the club. Garfield went to Keighley later on—he was an old man when he went—but the time I was playing for Amman he was with Neath. Garfield started on the wing with Amman and he'd played at Neath a couple of seasons and was always mentioning my name to the committee. They used to ask him how heavy I was and Garfield would add on a couple of pounds. Neath always said I was too light, you know, so Garfield lied about me. In the end it paid off.

One Friday night I was at home with mother. It was just before Christmas and there was a knock at the door. It was Garfield with a telegram in his hand. 'Bring the boy with you next Saturday', it said. Neath were playing Bridgend at Bridgend. In those days you had to have three signatures, each from an Amman United committee man, to get your permit. But we got them alright. After that we made the arrangement to meet on Saturday. Garfield came from Glanaman but he lived in Brynaman. As I left him he said, 'Be on the number nine bus tomorrow by The Half Moon and I'll meet you on the Waun. Bring your boots, that's all'. I did as I was told and hopped onto one of those old buses. You know the ones, with the steps outside? Old fashioned, they were.

I played the game with Bridgend and we made a draw and I remember it rained, teemed down. I'll never forget it. Afterwards

Evan Davies, Jack Davies (Dai's brother) and Garfield Phillips, after they signed for Keighley in September 1926. Garfield and Jack received £250 and Evan £150.

Neath R.F.C., 1924-25. Back Row: C. Heard (Committee), A. L. David (Secretary), W. B. Jones (Committee), F. David (Committee), Sergeant W. Hopkins (Committee), A. J. Mills (Committee). Second Row: J. Morris (Committee), G. Edwards, D. Pascoe, S. Daymand, M. Cole, P. Jones, D. R. Jenkins, T. Evans, M. Davies, D. Phillips, T. Arthur. Third row: D. R. Edwards (Committee), A. E. Freethy (Committee), W. J. Davies, T. Bevan, G. Phillips, P. Howells (Chairman), D. Hiddlestone (Captain), I. Jones, I. Davies, G. Morgan, H. Thomas, T. Davies (Vice Chairman), W. B. Morgan. Front Row: E. Williams, D. M. Davies.

I said to Garfield, 'What am I going to ask for expenses? What do I say for travelling to Neath?' 'Oh', says Garfield, 'ask for ten bob. Make it ten shillings'. So after the game they called me into the Neath office and there was the Sec., a Mr. David. I'll never forget him, little fella with a wax moustache. He said, 'How much do I owe you, D.M.?' I looked at him and I said , 'Oh, eleven bob'. I added a shilling. I was a cheeky bugger and blooming awkward, even in those days.

After the game we were having chicken and a bone got stuck in my throat. I suppose I was eating too quick. I turned to Garfield and told him I was choking. Garfield said, 'Come down to the toilet'. He put his finger in my mouth and down it went. Then Garfield said, 'Eat plenty of bread'. I did. After a bit I felt nothing of it. Just a little bone, that's all it was. I wonder now if it was a message sent down from the fella upstairs for asking the Sec. for that extra shilling. Eleven bob in expenses was a hell of a lot. You can get to be greedy once too often.

The next game was a midweek match against Ebbw Vale. I played a blinder. First half I got the ball, ran to the right and caught them all off balance. Then I switched left. There was a fella from Ammanford having a trial with us, a centre, Maldwyn Williams (he's dead and buried now). I ran to the fullback, gave it to Maldwyn and he scored under the posts. 'Thanks, Dai', he said. In the second half I crossed the line, say about three or four yards from the corner flag, but I wasn't satisfied. Nobody tackled me so I went over the line and started running towards the goal posts. I beat three men in the dead ball area. You know what I mean? I shouldn't have done it and they could have picked me up and carried me over the dead ball line. They could easily have stopped me from scoring, especially a big forward. But I beat them, the lot of them, and I put the ball down under the post.[1] I remember Dan Pascoe coming up to me. 'Well you cheeky little bugger, Davies', he said. So I winked at him. You know what I mean? I was having good fun and having good money. Enjoying myself.

Three pound a week from Neath I was getting. And over at times. In fact, I was better off down here than I was with Broughton. I was on the losing side at Broughton. It narked me. I used to get tired when I first went north and the fellas playing stand off were hopeless, you know. At Broughton Rangers losing money was thirty bob. With Neath whether we lost or not I was having three quid. At least three quid. And then, on top, I was earning good money in the Gelli Ceidrim. Over eight quid a week altogether. That's a lot of brass for a lad. When my brother and I were in the big vein we were earning up to thirteen pound a week all told. Unbelievable, when you think of it.

As for rugby, it's no use them saying they don't get paid. The idea of it! At Neath we used to march in to the Sec. The Captain would go in first, you know, Dai Hiddlestone from Hendy. Dai was Terry Price's grandfather and he played for Wales. In 1924 it was him who led the Welsh in their war dance when they played the New Zealanders. He got in big trouble and was hauled over the coals for taking the mickey out of the haka. But what a lad. 'Alright, boys', he'd say after a game. 'What are we waiting for? Let's get paid. Neath can afford it'.

There were huge crowds then, much bigger crowds than what you see today. The only crowd you see today is the Llanelli one. At Neath we used to strip in a club called The Bird in Hand, then walk to the field across the fairground. The Bird in Hand—I don't know whether it's on its feet now or not—I don't think it is. Anyway, they had shower baths

Jack Bassett, the Penarth and Wales Rugby Union full back, whom Dai ran rings round.

Mel Rosser, another Penarth star.

and towels, everything was there for us. We always made sure we played a good game.

After Ebbw Vale I was picked to play against Newport and then in the third match we had a midweek fixture at Penarth. Penarth had a few internationals in those days. Mel Rosser, a centre who went to Leeds. And Jack Bassett, a hulking fullback who captained Wales. Jack was a real big fella, policeman I think. In fact, Penarth were really a team of policemen and a lot went north. Jack Bassett finished as an inspector in the police at Bridgend. Arthur Bassett, his brother, was a winger. He went to Halifax and toured Australia—the same time as Ted Ward. But Jack was older.

So anyway, at Penarth, here we were. The field is on its side, you know, little slope. And here am I. I had to come out on leave from the pit but the ground was dry and it suited me. There were three of us from Amman United playing with Neath. Tom Evans, he's dead and buried now—I was in his funeral party. Tom was about six foot. He was amateur heavyweight boxing champion of Great Britain, army chap you know. And Garfield Phillips from Garnant. He was on the left wing. I was scrum half and having a great game. I remember going blind. I used to love going blind, you know. Bit of scope. I made this break and I was looking for Garfield but I was far too fast. He couldn't keep up with me and he was a wing. I remember seeing Jack Bassett in front of me, huge chap. It seemed like the players stood still for a second, just stood there and watched me run at Bassett between the twenty-five yard and the try line. It was no contest. I swerved around him, captain of Wales, and the fella he was looking for, nowhere to be seen. A shimmy, a swerve and there he was sprawled in a heap and me gone missing under the posts. I remember Pascoe coming up to me.

Dan went to Leeds from Neath. He was a good forward—second row—and he could kick goals. 'D.M.', he said. That's what they used to call me then. 'D.M., if I miss this, I want shooting'. He didn't, of course, and we licked Penarth by 30 odd points. Afterwards, I could hear the Neath officials saying, 'We'll have to sign him on now or somebody else will have him'. See? So they signed me on. And when Mr. David said afterwards, 'How much do we owe you?' I told him straight: two pound fifteen. From then on I was never dropped. Two pound fifteen was a big pick up for me. But I knew I was worth it. I wasn't big but I was full of tricks. The next season we went from strength to strength. We even broke Aberavon's ground record. Four years they were without losing a game but we put paid to it.

In Neath around Christmas time you have three matches like the Rugby League and you get more money. For us they were all at home, more or less. I remember one of the matches was London Welsh. At that time London Welsh had the Welsh half-backs playing for them. Windsor Lewis was stand off and W.C. Powell at scrum half. Powell was in the Welsh Guards and he was sponsored by some Captain Crawshay. Crawshay sponsored him, gave him coll. Powell was a big noise. Once he got picked on the wing against Scotland. They picked him on the wing, the right wing, to mark Ian Smith. Smith could gallop but, *Duw*... this fella, this W.C. Powell, he used to go up and knock hell out of Smith. It didn't matter if he had the ball or not, Powell would give this Smith a dig. Anyway, when we played London Welsh I said to myself, I'm stopping Powell. He's not scoring. But by damn he did. When I played against him he could throw a ball. Oh damn, he was a good player. And tough you know—big compared with me. Only thing

was he couldn't catch hold of me. Not that day. Powell might have scored but I scored as well. After the game an old scrum half of Neath who used to be the trainer came up to me in the bar. 'D.M.', he said. 'You beat him today. W.C. Powell, I mean. You beat him'. I was glad to hear him say that. W.C. Powell had far too big an opinion of himself. I mean, he used to carry a stack of cards with his name printed on and if a boy came up and asked him for an autograph he'd pull out a card from his inside pocket. Well, I ask you, what kind of a stunt is that to pull?

There were two top scrum halves when I played for Neath. W.C. Powell and Bob Delahay of Cardiff. Delahay came from Bridgend and was capped for Wales. They scattered his ashes on the Brewery Field. Delahay was a drinker, you know, but damn he was a good scrum half. He used to run with the ball. I like a scrum half that runs with the ball. I always say if you want to be a good player go and watch the best. If you are not playing one day go and watch how the other fella does it. In those days the international matches were held at Swansea as well as at Cardiff. It was done so those that lived in West Wales could get a chance to see the team. That's how I got to watch Bob Delahay and see what his strengths were. I knew he could run. But I also knew he couldn't catch me. And he didn't. The last match I played for Neath was at Cardiff Arms Park. I was far too quick for Delahay that day. That's why I did alright up north. [2]

You had to be tricky in the Rugby League. You had to use brains. Scrum half was the worst position of any to get into. Putting the ball in and retiring and all that. When I started I was being penalized umpteen times for being offside. At the scrum I used to jump on the other fella's back. You don't do that in Rugby League. You retire. In Rugby Union it's easier. I mean to say, you have wing forwards and the ball is there. Look at how they push and then carry the ball with them in the back row. The scrum half just follows it and they can't blooming tackle you. You've got plenty of time. You didn't have that time when I played Rugby League. They used to come and kick your hands and you had to be quick. Then there are the moves and you play for money and if you win you get more. There's also the training. I never trained with Neath. I used to train here with the Amman United, keep myself fit, you know. There was no coaching at Neath or anything like that.

In the days when I played Rugby Union Newport were always a hard team to beat, and Aberavon. We broke Aberavon's ground record. They had a three or four year record, I think, and Johnny Ring had played for them. Johnny was a bit before me. He went north in about 1922. He could run could Johnny. As for Swansea, they were nothing —we licked them easy. I remember playing for Neath at Swansea. During the game Garfield Phillips—he married a girl from Brynaman and kept a pub called The Gwyn Hotel—well, Garfield tackled his opposite winger and knocked him flat, catapulted him onto his back. The lad was a student and he'd come from the college or something. Anyway, we were going off under the stand after the game and Garfield was in front and then Tom Evans and me at the tail. Tom was a boxer in the army and he was tall, six foot two at least, and he had a long reach. Glyn Stephens was there as well and he was on the committee. Glyn was in the main stand above us. As we were going off this fellow that Garfield flattened had hold of something. I don't know what it was but he tried to hit Garfield on the head. He must have over-reached himself because he missed Garfield completely. I was coming up and all of a sudden I saw Tom

Evans make a fist and hit this fellow. *Duw, Duw,* you could see the cut and the blood all over him. The Swansea committee had a go at Glyn up there in the stand but Glyn walked away from it. He was right to walk away. The boy had asked for it good and proper. And Tom had given it—by God he had.

He was a good worker in the mines was Tom. He worked in the same colliery as me and he slept in our house umpteen times. He was pally with my brother, Jack, who went to Wembley. Later on they made Tom Evans an overman. Tom was alright until things went wrong and then he got upset. He was supposed to have lost his temper on the face and punched some of the miners. The lads wouldn't work with him after that and Tom had to leave the colliery. I wasn't here then, I was up north. But it seems they had a meeting with a colliery agent in the church hall one Sunday afternoon. 'Well, boys', he said, 'if you don't work under this man there is only one alternative. And that is, I'll have to close the colliery'. Soon as he said this somebody at the back of the hall shouted out, 'Close the damn thing then. Close it'. But they didn't. Instead, they fired Tom and Tom landed back in the Gelli Ceidrim.

By the mid 1920s things weren't so good in the Gelli Ceidrim and it went downhill. In 1925 the pit was on the point of closing—a lot of damp in the workings. It was hard to save money. At Neath the bit of extra I got was pocket money and I gave my wages to my mother. My real aim was to go north. Dick Murphy always said, 'Don't give up, Dai. You watch, you'll be up north soon'. 'Don't be silly', I said. 'All right', said Dick. 'I tell you what I'll do. I'll bet you five bob you go north before the year's out'. 'O.K.', I said. 'You're on'. But if I'd had the opportunity to go there and then, I'd have given him the money ten times over.

Ammanford square with the bus station and arcade at the top. Here is where the Rugby League scout, on his way to Neath, was intercepted by Jack Leyshon.

Eventually it did happen. I remember a fella telling me about a conversation he'd had with a scout. This scout was going to watch Aberavon and he wanted a scrum half. He'd broken his journey in Ammanford and was going on the bus from there to Aberavon. He enquired of a fella called Jack Leyshon who played fullback for the Amman and Ammanford.[3] Jack was a pretty good rugby player and he worked in the same colliery as me but was a lot older. Jack was under the veranda where the bus stop was and this scout got talking to him. 'Yes', he said. 'I'm going to watch a scrum half who plays for Aberavon'. Jack Leyshon told me this, years after, see. 'Oh', said Jack. 'You going to watch him? I've played against him. I wouldn't waste my time if I were you. Why don't you break your journey in Neath? There's a boy at Neath who's ten times better than that clown at Aberavon'. It appeared the scout took his advice and watched me instead.

He must have liked what he saw because soon after that they all started coming. I was playing pretty well. I reckon I could have had my cap if I'd stayed. The problem was, I was trapped in the mines and I wanted out. I was sick of the mines. When I signed for Broughton I got three hundred and fifty, a lot of money in those days. Exactly half of what the great Jim Sullivan got when he signed from Cardiff. Jim was only seventeen. So that gives you an idea of how good he was.

NOTES

1 In a report of the Amman v Ystalyfera game in 1924 'Atlas' describes Dai as 'exceptionally clever beating his opponent time after time but much of his play was spoilt through his tendency to hold on too long'. *Amman Valley Chronicle,* 6 November 1924.

2 The *Evening Post,* 25 January 1926, says that Delahey 'failed to shine when in direct opposition to D.M. Davies'.

3 Jack Leyshon was on the committee of Ammanford Rugby League. A fascinating insight into the tensions that existed within the club is provided by the *Amman Valley Chronicle,* 24 July 1913. It reports a committee meeting which took place at the Cross Inn Hotel in which Jack Leyshon opposed the proposal of the Chairman, Jim Derbyshire, to strike Amman United from the Ammanford fixture list for rough play.

3: The Ways of the English

It was a fella from Ammanford who took me north. He worked with my wife's father in the colliery in Garnant. His name was Trevor Evans, same name as the international and he married Dai Edwards' sister from Glynneath. She was a widow and Dai played for Rochdale. Dai was a second row forward with Glynneath and a Welsh international. He's one of the few that's been capped for Wales while playing second class.

Trevor Evans was a scout for Broughton. He didn't know a sausage about rugby but he took me to Broughton, along with Jack Elwyn Evans and Evan Phillips. Jack Elwyn and Evan Phillips were signed the week before me. I should have gone with them but I was supposed to be going on tour to Devon. I went the week after. As it turned out I could have gone earlier as the tour was cancelled owing to the snow.

I had never been out of Wales before. When I saw Crewe with all the lines and the platforms I was amazed. We changed at Crewe and went to Manchester. From there we took a tram, big trams in Manchester they were. Broughton's ground was near to Manchester race course. The River Irwell separated it from the race track. These days it's called The Cliff and Manchester United have it as a training ground.

I didn't know anything of the players, no-one at all. It was hard work, I can tell you. My English was weak, about as weak as the rugby Broughton were playing. They had one international, that's all, a wing who'd toured Australia. Billy Bentham his name was. And he went back a long way.

In the trial we got beat.[1] We played

The earliest known photograph of Dai Davies in Broughton kit.

Widnes and I got a black eye. I remember they wanted to sign me on as soon as the game was over. I walked straight into the directors room. The directors were sat down. 'We'll give you three hundred and fifty', they said straight off. I nodded my head. I was really green. I didn't think about a contract. I didn't think about anything. I didn't even ask for more than three fifty. I just signed the

Broughton Rangers' ground at The Cliff was opened in September 1913 and could hold 50-60,000 spectators. In this 1931 shot, Broughton are playing Wigan in a Lancashire Cup game. Manchester United took over the facilities as a training ground.

Dai and Jack, in what looks like Broughton kit.

contract and got my money. I don't know what Jack, my brother, got at Keighley but I don't think he had as much as me.[2]

There were a lot of Welshmen up north during the time I was there. In the 1930s Wigan almost had a team of Welshmen. When I played they had Johnny Ring and Tommy Parker. Tommy spoke Welsh and Johnny spoke English. Then there was Billo Rees at Swinton. I played with Billo for Wales and we used to talk a lot in Welsh. I used to say everything in Welsh to Billo and the other fellas didn't know what the hell we were talking about. When I went to Warrington I was one of seven from Wales. Funny thing is, I was the only Welsh speaker. The others came from places like Ebbw Vale. They spoke English there, see. Even if they came from Swansea they often spoke English— most did anyway. Those of us who came from Llanelli and Ammanford always spoke Welsh when we got together. It was like being at home. In Glanaman I'd been one of five brothers and two sisters and we all spoke Welsh. My mother spoke Welsh … couldn't write in English. They didn't have much education then. Not like now. Now they're at school and at home you hear them speak in English.

I found it difficult at Broughton. I was in digs and I had to speak English all the time. It was all English. I said to Jack Elwyn, 'I don't know what to say. What shall I call the old man?' 'Call him dad', said Jack. 'And what about the old lady?' 'Call her ma', said Jack. 'Dad and ma'. So I did. That was easy for me, see.

I soon got used to speaking English and I was well looked after. Match days, I had a boiled egg with the landlady and then I'd catch the tram. If we were playing away I would get the tram into Manchester, catch the train at Victoria Station and have lunch going out—steak, you see. Then we would land in whatever town we were playing and if it was only a mile or so from the station and the weather was fine we'd walk it to the ground to get relaxed. After the game—win, lose or draw—we'd come back to the station. The food was good on the train but I could never eat much. I was usually jiggered— played out. The first thing the trainer would do with the chaps who were cooking the meals was order me two bottles of Guinness. That would give me an appetite. Then I would eat along with the others. If we were late landing back in Broughton it was back to the digs with Jack Elwyn and straight into bed. I wasn't married then.

Broughton was hard work. I had to create the openings and score the tries.[3] With Warrington it was different. They could finish the moves. I never got what I deserved at Broughton. You soon found out what the lads at the other clubs were getting. You'd meet in a pub and talk about it. Even if you were at loggerheads on the field you were good friends off it. We used to talk and say, 'Well how much do you get then?' That kind of thing. If you were playing your guts out and getting nowhere, like me at Broughton, you looked for a move to a better club.

It was my second season at Broughton when I got all my teeth knocked out. It was just before Christmas and we were away at Widnes.[4] I remember we were beating them 13-0 and I was about to go over for a try from the scrum. There was this fellow, Crompton his name was, a fair-haired chap. He hit me with a punch—nearly knocked me out.[5] I got up and started running—anywhere—then my tongue came into contact with all my bottom teeth. The gums were flattened. I could feel them. The trainer put a small sponge in my mouth and pulled the teeth back. I had to go off the field. Afterwards, I had a gold plate holding the teeth but they started to decay. It wasn't long before I had them extracted. A dentist in Warrington made me a protector. But that didn't last long. I was playing Wakefield at Wakefield and I was going across to pick up the ball. In came a swiper. It smashed the rubber holding the plates, top and bottom. I never wore it after that.

I needed a break from Broughton and during the time of the General Strike I came home for the summer.[6] My father hadn't broke the home up then so I was still in Glanaman. There was a sports day on the park down here. In the final of the sprint, the hundred yards, I beat Jack Elwyn and gave the prize money to the unemployed. There were three lads mending shoes on the park, so I gave it to them. I also gave a pound towards the soup kitchens.

My brother Jack had come home before me—he was at Keighley—and I'd told him to enter me in the sprints as I was aiming for a

A carnival on the Amman ground similar to those that took place on Dai's summer holidays.

holiday. The prize was six pounds and a silver cup. I backed myself, 3-1 for a five pound stake. Jack put two pound on me as well. I knew I could do it. There was no jockey on my back. Up at Broughton I trained practically every day. I was the fastest man in Broughton's team and me the scrum half.

In my first heat I gave a yard and a half to a boy from Llanelli. Lance Fowler, brother of Ike Fowler who played wing for Llanelli. I ran past him from the start. Ran away with the heat. I remember Lance's father came up to me and asked if I was a professional runner. 'I am not a professional runner', I said, 'I am a professional footballer'. 'Oh, soccer', he said. 'No, Rugby League. I play for Broughton'. 'What are you—a wing?' he said. 'No, scrum half'. 'Good God', he said. 'What is the wing like up there if you're the scrum half?' So I told him. 'I can lick any of them in the team', I said. 'I'm not a big man, but I can lick them'. 'Well then', he said, 'I'll back you in the semi final'. I won that one as well and then the final. I didn't let him down.

I won twenty-one pound that day between the fifteen pound I bet on myself and the six quid prize. The following year I did it again. This time I ran in the 220 yards. Jack Elwyn ran in the quarter mile. He knew he couldn't beat me in the 100 yards—and him a cap with the Rugby Union. Of course I didn't smoke or nothing and I didn't drink much. Only a Guinness now and again. I looked after myself.

Back at Broughton it was tough. When I first went north I went with my eyes closed. I was getting more money playing for Neath. At Broughton I was on three pound for a win and thirty bob for a lose and I was on the losing end nearly every time. I played my guts out and got browned off. I didn't even have a job. With Neath you got three pound whatever the result, and with the work in the pit, even as a joiner's mate, I was bringing home over eight pounds a week. Broughton were skinflints. Their directors were breaking us. The crowds were small and they had no money.

At Christmas they told us they were going to cut our wages even more.[7] We were supposed to be playing the touring New Zealanders at Broughton. But when we heard the news, Evan Phillips, Jack Elwyn and myself jumped on a train and came back home. The papers were full of it. 'Welshmen gone home', it said. 'Welshmen on strike'. We didn't care what they said in the papers. We were determined to stick to our guns. And we were right to do so.

It wasn't long before there was a telegram at the house. It came from the Sec. at Broughton. Hoey, his name was. The telegram told me to come to the 'phone at a certain time. I decided I would use the chemist's shop in Garnant. The chemist, Dai Evans, used to enjoy watching me play. He went to the same chapel as me and he had a son who's a doctor—living below here [8] but he's retired. Anyway, it was the chemist who put me through to Broughton.

Kennedy it was—Kennedy the Chairman who was on the other end. 'I am fed up', I said. 'I am fed up killing myself for you'. Kennedy said, 'Now look here, Dai. Don't stand in your own light. We'll arrange things for you. We don't want the other two back, but we want you. And we'll give you more than you had before'. 'Hang on a minute', I said and I put the phone down. The other two lads were with me. I'd told them to be there. I didn't want to do anything underhanded, you know. Evans the chemist had gone out the back so I said to Jack Elwyn and Evan Phillips, 'They don't want you back. Do you understand me?' The lads stood there. They were stunned, you know. Didn't know what to say. So I picked the phone up. 'Listen now', I said. 'I am not coming back. I am not coming unless the other two come with me. And we all want the same money—the same money as I get'. 'What money is that?' said Kennedy. So I told him. 'A damn sight more than what we had before'. After a lot of blowing Kennedy agreed. I wasn't going to stand for bullying from him.

We went back but it wasn't long before I quarrelled again. They started with the same old caper about cropping our money and this time I decided I would go for good. When I told them what I thought they called me in. 'You're knocking pounds off me', I said. 'If this carries on I'll be playing for nothing. How do you expect me to pay for my digs? You'd better put me on the transfer'. I remember a new director was there, Major Hampson, First World War chap. He was jumping up all the time I was speaking. I wasn't good at English, you know, speaking Welsh at home, and I wasn't clear what everyone was saying. I was struggling to understand. This Hampson fella was jumping up and down like a turkey cock and calling me Davies. I wasn't taking that so I stood up as well. 'Now listen', I said. 'Cut that out. There's a handle to my name and you either call me Dai or Mr. Davies. I am not in school now, you know. And I'm not in the army either. You may have been in charge of the soldiers but you are not in charge of me. I am the captain. I am the boss. Without me or the other players you would be nothing'. I remember Kennedy stepped in. Building contractor and Chairman of the club. 'Who do you think you are?' he said. 'We made you. Don't you forget that'. 'You made me?' I said. 'Don't talk silly. How did Broughton ever make me? I made myself. It had nothing to do with you or Broughton. And if that's your attitude you can put me on the transfer'. 'That's for the Board to decide', roared Kennedy. So I walked out.

The following morning I was on the transfer. I saw it on the poster outside the digs in the newsagent shop. BROUGHTON STAR ON LIST, it read.

Dai, as he may have looked, when Broughton put him on the 'list'.

I was relieved. I knew I could find a club. I could go to Hull. Hull were the best paying club in the rugby league at the time. Seven pound for a win, six pound for a draw, five pound for a lose. We played at Hull in the second round of the Rugby League cup in February 1927. We were beating them 10-0 and I made the openings for two tries. Then Evan Phillips, the number thirteen, got a blow on the head and didn't know where he was. He had to go off and we were a man short. We didn't have subs like you have them today. All we had were five forwards. I had to play scrum half as well as loose forward and watch the blind side. When Phillips went off, damn, they started scoring. Clawed their way back. We were hanging on by our fingertips. Suddenly we had a scrum between the twenty five and the try line, our half of the field. It was my put in so I shoved it under the forwards feet—anything to get it back. We were losing by that stage—twenty points to ten I think it was—and when I got the ball I went to the open. I ran like hell, beat them all including the fullback and scored under the posts. I must have run about eighty or ninety yards. It was a heck of a good try, if I say so myself. I remember the old man, Bill Whykert. He was a trainer or groundsman at Broughton Rangers. Bill thought the world of me and I stayed in his digs. I remember coming back from Hull with him on the train. 'Dai-a', he said, 'Dai-a, they're after you now. Hull want you. I heard them say it to the Broughton directors. "How much do you want for Davies, the scrum half?"'

I could have joined Hull if I'd wanted. I could have joined Emlyn Gwynne from Gowerton and W.J. Davies and Edgar Morgan from Llanelli. In those days I could have gone anywhere Hull, Leeds, Oldham. They all came for me. Oldham even offered me a pub. And if my mother had been alive I'd have gone to Oldham. I'd have brought them all up—my mother, father, sister, brother. By that stage my mother had died and my father had split the home up.

I could even have gone to Wigan. The directors came and I remember what they said. 'Jim will put you right', they said—meaning the great Jim Sullivan. I didn't like them saying that, not after Broughton. I said to myself, no Jim's going to put me right. I'm going to put myself right. And I did. I made sure of it.

I asked Broughton what transfer I was on. They weren't supposed to tell me, you know, but they did. Eight hundred and fifty pounds, they said. It was a big sum. Especially in those days. In fact, I was almost the first thousand pound transfer. Stanley Brogden was really the first. He went to Huddersfield from Bradford Northern for over a thousand pounds. But I damn near beat him. I was great pals with Stanley. By God he could run. He was the fastest centre I ever saw. He wasn't big but he could gallop. He was often in the Powderhall Sprints in Scotland.

After Wigan there was Warrington and two directors came to the house. Their names were Jack Oddy and Jack Knowles. The son of the landlady—Albert we called him—answered the door. Albert was a bit disabled and he came in to fetch me. As I walked down the stairs I could hear this pair talking to each other while Albert was stood there. 'Who's that?' said Jack Oddy pointing to Albert at the bottom of the stairs. 'Why, it's Phillips the loose forward', said Jack Knowles. 'Is he injured?' said Jack Oddy. 'No', said Knowles. 'He's always like that'. Oddy looked back at him. 'No bloody wonder they lose every game',

On the following Saturday—the middle of November it was—we were playing Wigan in a league match. There were two lads from

Warrington on trial at Broughton—Holland, a stand off, and Stowell, the fullback. According to Jack Oddy and Jack Knowles they were going to be part of the transfer deal. In other words, if I'd sign for Warrington they'd come to Broughton. 'Listen, Dai', said Jack Oddy. 'Play a bad game Saturday'. 'Why?' I said. Oddy looked at me like I was simple. 'Why do you think? To bring down your transfer fee, of course'. That wasn't on. I couldn't go on the field at Broughton and not pull my weight. And that's what I told them. In the event I played a blinder and we beat Wigan 10-8. Wigan were a star-studded team at the time. I may even have scored, I can't remember. I certainly made one for the stand-off Tommy Wilson.

On the following Friday I was asked to go up to Warrington. On the Thursday, however, the Oldham directors came to Broughton and told me they were going to sign me the following Saturday and take me back with them. When Friday came I travelled to Warrington with my pal Garfield Phillips and we all met up in the directors' room under the stand.

I was sticking out for two hundred and fifty of a backhander and Garfield spoke up for me. He told the committee men that if Warrington didn't sign me there and then they'd lose me for good as I was going to Oldham the following morning. It seemed to do the trick. The directors got out the contract and told me to sign. It was all spelled out. A suitable job on the ground. Four pound a week guaranteed with my wages to be made up to four pound if the job I was doing paid less. That, plus two hundred and

A classic shot of Dai in Warrington strip.

fifty in my back pocket. I wasn't supposed to get a backhander—it was against the rules of the Rugby League—but I did. I suppose, if you look at it that way, I was the first unofficial thousand pound transfer.

NOTES

[1] The *Amman Valley Chronicle* reports his performance in the trial as 'brilliant'. *Amman Valley Chronicle,* 4 February 1926. The *Daily Dispatch* says that the trial game was against Wigan Highfield not Widnes. *Daily Dispatch,* 24 November 1927. Dai's first club game after his signing was against Widnes.

[2] Jack's signing-on fee was reported as £250.

[3] This is confirmed by match reports in the *Salford City Reporter,* which regularly describes Dai's play as 'brilliant', 'cavalier', 'polished' and 'admirable'. The *Daily Dispatch* which also covered Broughton's matches, commonly refers to Dai Davies as a player who 'introduced a lot of life' into a game. He is often commended for his ability to break from the base of the scrum and varied tactics.

[4] 11 December 1926. Broughton lost 13-25.

[5] This match was played on 11 December 1926. The *Salford City Reporter* of 11 December 1926 says that 'Up to the time of his injury Davies had been the best half on the field'. The following week Dai returned to Garnant with Evan Phillips and Jack Elwyn Davies.

[6] It appears that Dai was a fine cricketer and whilst at home played for the Prospect Stars Cricket Team. The *Amman Valley Chronicle* refers to him as a 'fine, all round athlete, [who] at cricket is equally at home as in football and swimming'. *Amman Valley Chronicle,* 24 June 1926.

[7] The local newspapers report that Broughton players were asked to forfeit a months wages in order to bail the club out of financial difficulties. It also suggests that Dai was one of the ground staff and was made redundant.

[8] Dai is referring to his own home in New School Road, Garnant. This is where all conversations and recordings took place.

4: Live Wire

I never regretted signing for Warrington. They treated me well and I got my international cap the first year I was there. I played at Wembley five times, with four runner up medals and I won three Lancashire cup medals. I didn't tour Australia but not because I wasn't good enough. There was another reason, but I don't want to go into it at the moment.

Warrington was a nice ground. It was always packed. It could hold between 35,000 and 40,000 and Wigan about 50,000. There was no soccer team, only rugby in Warrington, and the Rugby Union team was nil. They all came to watch us. We were the idols of the town.

I remember a little boy by the name of Jackie Ditchfield. He was a cripple and he lived not far from where I was lodging. I used to see him in a wheelchair being pushed to the ground. Jackie watched every game and they used to bring him in and leave the wheelchair under the stand, on the right-hand side. I must have been the boy's idol because he sent

Warrington R.L.F.C. were Lancashire Cup Winners in 1932-33, beating St. Helens 10-9. Dai Davies and Tommy Thompson scored the tries. Front Row: Dai, Jack 'Cod' Miller, Jackie Oster, Nat Bentham, B. Shankland (Captain).

A Good Friday crowd for the Warrington game against Widnes in the 1920s. Note the wheelchair.

me a letter with an autograph book. He asked me if I would go round the players and ask them to fill their names in the book. He also said if I would come out of the tunnel at our next home match and walk to the right and wave to him. I didn't know what to do. So I asked the captain, Nat Bentham.[1] Nat read the letter and said, 'You come out behind me next Saturday. I'll have the ball and you run towards the right and then I'll give you a long pass. Kick it or do anything you want then wave to him'. And that's just what I did. It wasn't much, I suppose. But the lad must have been in high jinks when I did it.

They were proud of me in Warrington. I worked there on the ground with Nat Bentham, Billy Holding and Tommy Flynn. We were miners and one of the first jobs they had us do was dig a hole under the stand to make a tunnel to the dressing room. I remember later on they signed a forward from New Zealand, Rex King his name was, and the morning they brought him to the ground we were stood by the tunnel. Tommy Flynn had a spirit level and the *Warrington Guardian* were taking photographs. Rex King stood on the terrace with Billy Bennett, the trainer, and they came and stood by the members' gate. 'What do you think of them?' said Billy pointing to us. There were four of us, see.

Dai and Nat Bentham put the finishing touches to the tunnel at Warrington.

this'. And he got the tape out and put it round me. Then he put it round the New Zealander. I was ten stone six or ten stone seven. I don't remember. But I do remember I was an inch and a half bigger than King around the chest. 'That's our lightest boy', said Billy. And he laughed. Rex King said nothing. He had the shock of his life.

Warrington worked at building you up. When I came back home people would always remark how big I'd got. There was a fellow worked with me in Pantyffynnon. Glyn Morris his name was. He played for Pontardulais, came from Hendy but lived in Pen-y-groes. Worked in Canada with my brother Will. I don't know whether he's dead now or not but he always used to tell people about me. I remember him telling the mobile people with the X-rays. 'You know', he said, 'There was more meat on a greasy fork than there was on Dai before he went north. And now look at him. Look at his chest. Look what they've done'. That was Glyn Morris. He talked like that.

I enjoyed Warrington. The atmosphere was great. After the game Jess Meredith and me would go to a restaurant or a pub. We were good pals and we'd have a drink or two with our wives. The people would shout, 'Hullo, Jess, Hullo, Dai'. Things like that. And we would wait in the pub and they'd say, 'It won't be long now, Jess'. Then the sandwiches would come and we used to tuck in and we didn't need any supper at all that night.

I liked playing for Warrington. On the Thursday team sheet I was always first choice. It was automatic, see. There was no bad feeling. The players were friendly. Not like the team I went to at Huddersfield. Huddersfield were no good. I didn't like the trainer they had. I didn't like his methods. He was a big head. He'd played for Hudders-

Tommy and me were the same height, but not tall. Nat, being a hooker, was a squat fellow. Billy Holding, the fullback, was the tallest among us. 'Oh, they're a puny lot', said Rex King. He didn't know we were players. Billy looked at us and winked. 'I'll show you how puny', said Billy and he beckoned me over. 'Come here, Dai', he said. 'I want you for a minute'. I walked over and jumped the concrete wall surrounding the ground. 'Come into the dressing room, will you?' said Billy. 'I want you to strip'. 'What for?' I said. 'I'm not going training. That's tonight'. 'I don't want you to train', said Billy. 'Take your top off, that's all'. Billy used to make a showman of me. 'Now', said Billy to Rex King when we got inside, 'Watch

field in that great team they had in 1912. A centre he was—Edgar Wrigley, a white New Zealander.

Warrington were completely different. At training night they would have you in your spikes and you would go round the track, deep breathing. You were always with a couple of men, three or four of you trotting, and you wouldn't think anything of sprinting round the track. You would be in the trainer's hands, see, and he would have you on the cinder track sprinting, but he wouldn't put us down in the holes like a sprinter. There was too much strain there, see. Instead, we ran two or three together and he would shout 'go' and you would let fly and sprint for about fifty yards and die out like an alarm clock and walk back, deep breathing. At night they had these lights on and he used to send us inside and we would put our socks and boots on and come out again. Tick and pass we used to play, across the width of the field.

Some of the players went swimming but I didn't bother. Swimming makes your muscles stiff when they have to be loose. You don't see sprinters like Carl Lewis swimming. In my opinion swimming does something to the muscles if you're a runner. I don't know what it is. I used to swim a bit, but I wasn't very good and I didn't do a lot of it.

I learned as much as I could at Warrington. The trainer, Bill Bennett,[2] used to put two sticks in the ground with a couple of strings across. Then he'd go to the other side of the sticks and play the ball back to me and I used to scoop it up and go under the strings left and right, left and right. It was good practice for when I got the ball at acting half back or out of the scrum. I learned to duck and go like a rocket.

Warrington R.L.F.C. 1930-32. Nat Bentham, Captain. Back row, second left is Charlie Seeling Jr, son of the great 1905 All Black and Wigan Rugby League player (see later illustration). Dai is kneeling, front left.

Billy Bennett, the Warrington trainer.

In Rugby League you learn as you go along. You learn the moves. At Warrington we had marvellous moves. They were almost as good as the ones at Swinton. Jackie Oster and I used to practise them. If we were pressing in a game I used to say 'Come on up, Jackie'.

I remember one game at St. Helens. They had a helluva good side. Alf Ellaby, Tommy Frodsham, Leslie Fairclough. We got the ball from the scrum. I passed long toward Jackie and ran toward him. By the time the ball reached Jackie he'd advanced one or two steps and turned his back to the opposition. I came along and grabbed hold of the ball from Jackie and shot through the gap. No one saw me. I remember another game against Barrow at Warrington. There was a scrum

Jess Meredith hands off as Billy Holding, Dai Davies and Charlie Seeling move up in support.

on the left. Tommy Flynn was the stand off.[3] When he wanted to go on a dummy run Tommy used to drop his hand the opposite way to fool their backs. Three times he did that. The wingman, 'Fanny' Roberts we called him, scored twice from that move. I got the ball from the scrum, ran and dummied Tommy who was going in the opposite direction to me. They all took the dummy and ran after Tommy. I went toward the touchline and passed inside to Perkins, the centre, and he gave the ball to Fanny who scored in the corner. Same thing happened at Hull K.R. I went blind to the left. Their scrum half—sturdy fella—plus the loose forward and the fullback, all followed me. I passed inside to Charlie Seeling and he was in under the posts. I did it without looking. I used to practise that move so many times.

We once had a trial match and I played opposite a scrum half from Oldham. He wouldn't retire at the scrum and kept kicking my fingers. The next scrum I held onto the ball instead of passing to Tommy Flynn just so the scrum half would have to tackle me. As he came in I turned and swivelled and caught him in the face with my hips. They carried him off. We never saw him again.

I can't say I was a dirty player. I always thought of myself as fair. In thirteen years I got sent off once. We were playing Swinton at Swinton. It was during the first half and we got a ball from the scrum. It came out quick and I had to run back for it. Tommy Flynn was facing me and I picked up the ball and passed it to him. Their scrum half came after me and as I passed to Tommy this fellow opposite gave me a jab. I turned round and gave him a back hander. There we stood and I hit this fellow about three or four times with some lefts. I was taller than him, see. The referee came between us, turned us round

What looks like a planned move between Dai Davies and Charlie Seeling.

This seemed to be an in-joke at Warrington in the 1930s. A number of photographs in Warrington museum show players sitting on each others knees.

Players reunion, from left to right: Billy Kirk, Leslie Perkins and Dai Davies.

and sent the pair of us off. When I was going to the tunnel I said to this fellow, 'Come on then', I said. 'We'll finish it off under the stand, just you and me'. But he wouldn't have it. I remember the crowd, they threw clinker at me. I had to run like hell. Afterwards, the rugby league gave me a one match suspension. It was the only blemish on my football career.

Warrington were an outstanding team and I played with them for eight or nine seasons. My first game was at Wigan Highfield. It was a good game and I played with the likes of Tommy Flynn, Arthur Frowen, Billy Rhodes and Jim Tranter.

At the end of the 1927-8 season I played in my first cup final. We played Swinton and the game was at Wigan in the days before the rugby league went to Wembley. Swinton were a great side. They'd won all the cups that year but they were blooming lucky to beat us. I played on the wing opposite Chris Brockbank.[4] Warrington didn't have a wing but they had two scrum halves. One played for England—Billy Kirk from Wigan—so they asked me would I go on the wing. I'd already played on the wing in the semi final against Leeds at Rochdale when we won 9-2.

In the first half Swinton were three points up when Billy Kirk got hurt. I'll never forget it. Billy was flat out and there was steam coming from him. He'd had a rabbit punch or something and he was steaming. There was a lot of fuss. Billy was a Catholic so they brought the priest on. They thought he was dead. Then they carried him off. I had to come in off the wing and play half back.

The first scrum was sensational. I broke through and put Charlie Seeling in at the corner. Now we were neck and neck, a try each, and it looked like a draw. There's no question we should have won the game. Tommy Flynn scored a fair try. So did I. I kicked through and touched the ball over the try line before it went dead but the try was disallowed. If we had held out for a draw the game would have been replayed and we'd have won easily. The touring team was going to Australia and Billo Rees, Bryn Evans and Jack Evans from Swinton, they'd all been selected. If there had been a replay they'd have been at sea.

It never got that far. There was a scrum. Swinton's put-in but we got the ball. I made a break and kicked to touch on the halfway. Instead of playing advantage the referee brought us back for a crooked feed. It was our put in but Swinton won the ball against the head. Swinton were playing their A team scrum half and he gave the ball to Jack Evans who dropped a goal. They beat us 5-3. It was a big disappointment. There were no subs in those days and after Billy Kirk went we played the second half with a man short.

Billy Dingsdale.

Things went from bad to worse after that. We lost every game for the rest of the season —every game except the last. We were away at Dewsbury and it looked like we were in for a good hiding. Warrington's directors, Ish Hackett and Ish Isherwood—the twins we called them—had brought only losing money. In the first half Dewsbury trounced us—tries and goals—and they had a good, goal-kicking forward. But in the second half we turned them round and Billy Rhodes was kicking goals from all over. I scored a try the full length of the field. Eventually we won the game and the two Ishes didn't know what to say. They certainly couldn't pay us. 'We haven't got the money', they said. 'You'll have to wait until Monday morning. We didn't bring enough'. And we did. It couldn't be helped. None of the lads made any fuss.

During my second season at Warrington I broke down with cartilage trouble. I went to see a specialist, Mr. Douglas, in Manchester. He told me I must go into hospital straight away and he would operate and extract the cartilage. I was in hospital about ten days. When I came out I was limping and there was swelling on my knee. The specialist told me I could walk and do exercises, but not severe. They took me to Warrington Infirmary, and I'll never forget it, they put my leg in a case surrounded by heat and plenty of lamps. Hell, I was sweating like a bull. I thought to myself, I am not coming here again. So I asked Warrington if I could go back home. I was staying with my sister in Ammanford and my father told me about a fellow in Brynaman. He was a punch ball expert and he was supposed to be a good masseur. I went to him and he rubbed my knee in oil and pulled it this way and that, but it made no difference. I went back to Warrington and I asked them if I could go to this fella I remembered from Trafford Park, Harry

Taylor, the masseur who'd looked after me when I played for Broughton. Harry used to follow Broughton and he wanted to teach me to be a masseur.

Harry was a great fellow. What a difference he made. I went to see him two or three times a week. I used to go to Old Trafford by train and tram and he would rub me down. Funny thing was he never touched my knee. He wanted the muscles to come back of their own accord. 'That's where the strength is', he said. He had a machine and it used to twist and turn the muscles above the knee, pull them around; it was really marvellous.

After a bit I could feel my leg improving and getting stronger and Harry said, 'I want you to go and start running, but not hard. Go and train with the boys, but don't try to follow them, lag behind. Put spikes on'. He also asked me to do a lot of walking. I did and after a few weeks he said I could play.

I remember they picked me for the first team. It was against Rochdale and a fellow from Glynneath was playing, Dai Edwards, the one I've already told you about. Dai was a forward, a Welsh international from down here. He'd played for a second-class side, I don't think it was ever done before. After the game Mr. Douglas came to see me and Harry Taylor, the masseur. My leg was sore, very sore as if it had been kicked. It hadn't been kicked and I told Dai Edwards how bad I felt. 'Don't worry about it', said Dai. 'Even if you were a crock on one leg', he said, 'we'd have you at Rochdale'.

After that I told Warrington to play me on the A team. They did and I was having first team money. That was the season when we won the Lancashire Combination. We never lost a game, home or away, and we were drawing bigger crowds than the first team. I don't know whether it was because I was playing. I could feel my leg getting better and better. At the end of the season we caught up with Swinton. We had the same number of points as them and we had to have a play off at Wigan. We beat them easy. I've still got the medal. It's like a Lancashire cup medal, exactly the same: same weight, same gold, same shield, same design. I am proud of that medal.

Warrington won the Lancashire Cup in 1929 and in 1932 when we beat St. Helens at Wigan. St. Helens were a good side in those days with Alf Ellaby and George Lewis. Jackie Oster, a lad from Wigan, played stand off half with me that day and him and me scored a beautiful try. We were passing to each other—reverse passing—'til I broke through a gap and went in under the posts. I think that year was my best ever and we got to the final of the Challenge Cup.

On the way to the final we played at Batley in the second round. It was a cramped, little ground and in the second half we played with the slope. The referee was Albert Harding. I knew him well. Albert was a good referee and he often trained with us at Broughton. Albert was great company. He knew if he told the Warrington club what his plans were they'd invite him along and give him the same type of grub as the players. Anyway, in the first half at Batley we didn't score a lot of points.

Albert Harding, the referee.

Come the second half they played the up and under game, but we held our own and scored a try. That broke their hearts. I think it was Billy Dingsdale who scored and I remember the crowd were on to Harding, calling him all sorts, including a crafty bastard. I could see Harding was getting worried. He blew his whistle and ordered a scrum near the stand where the dressing room and showers were. The crowd were terrible and I stuck by Candy Evans, the second row. Anyway, as the scrum came together, Harding comes up and he says to me, 'Listen, Dai. This is the last scrum. Do you understand? You put the ball in, and make sure you get it. When you have it, boot it as high as you can, and make sure it goes into touch'. I did as he told me. Soon as I got the ball I hoofed it right into the crowd. Harding blew his whistle for the end of the game and went like hell for the dressing rooms. We all stood there with our mouths open as Albert flew in under the stands. Never looked round. Afterwards, it said in the papers, 'Of all the players on the field at Batley, Albert Harding was the fastest man'.

Albert was a card. Whenever we played in Yorkshire you could bet he would pinch a lift at Victoria Station. What a character. On the train he often gave us a lively account of the games he'd refereed. I remember him saying how he once did a derby match between Hull and Hull Kingston. 'I had both packs in front of me', said Albert. 'And they were terrific. I remember in the scrums they were swearing like mad. I couldn't stand it any longer. So I said, 'Now look here, lads, if you don't stop this f'ing and blinding, you will either have me or the ball in the family way. The two packs broke up and started laughing. I had no more backchat after that', he said.

The next round of the cup we played Wigan away. Hector Gee was their scrum half and they also had Jack Morley from

Newport on the wing and Jim Sullivan at fullback. They had others playing for them who weren't that famous like Hal Jones, the prop. He was with Keighley when I went there later on and he managed a pub.

First off, Sullivan kicked a goal and Billy Holding replied. Then Jack Morley scored a try. I remember I cut him off and made him score near the corner flag to make it difficult for Jim. As luck would have it Jim missed the goal. For the rest of the match it was very close. All goal kicks. With only a few minutes to go we were losing seven points to four. The Warrington crowd were leaving the ground when Billy Holding got the ball. He booted it high in the air, followed up and put all our men on side. The ground was dry and the ball was bouncing between Hector Gee and Jim Sullivan. Charlie Seeling picked it up and gave it to Nat Bentham—both Wiganers playing for Warrington. I came flying up on the outside, like grease lightning, and shouted to the pair of them to give me the ball. I don't know whether it was Charlie or Nat but there it was, a lovely pass, and I can remember seeing the left hand flag at the Spion Kop end. I went for the corner. Sullivan was coming across but I was going diagonally and I beat him for speed and scored in the corner. As I touched down Sullivan booted me in the side but I didn't feel a thing. I'd scored in the corner and made the score seven points apiece.

The snow was on the ground and Billy Holding, our kicker, took the goal kick wide out. He put the ball right on the touchline and I held it for him. The goal posts at Wigan are higher than anywhere else in the Rugby League. They are a tremendous height. But Billy stood there, measured his step and kicked the ball right over the top. As he did the whistle went for the end of the game. I could see Jim Sullivan underneath with his

Billy Holding.

head in his hands. We'd won by two points, 9-7. I tried to get off but I was mobbed by the crowd. In fact, I was so late in coming in they closed the gates to the players' tunnel. I had to jump over the wall on the left and walk out with the crowd where the Douglas is.[5]

We got to Wembley that year and beat St. Helens in the semis. Before the final I got myself involved with a fella from Hunslet who used to make football boots. He came into the dressing room at Warrington and said, 'Which one is Dai Davies?' I answered him and he told me to take my shoes and

42

socks off and to stand on a piece of cardboard. Then he drew around each of my feet with a pencil, left and right. The fella was a bootmaker, Elmer Cotton his name was, and he'd had a partnership with a man called Oxford. They'd split up and Elmer was doing the boots on his own. Elmer gave me a pair of these boots. The Harry Waggy he called them, after the famous Huddersfield centre, Harold Wagstaff. These boots were like kidgloves, soft and light, but useless for playing rugby in. On heavy ground your toe used to come up through the front and hurt you. Stanley Smith wore them at Wakefield but I never bothered. I certainly didn't wear them at Wembley. Wembley was a spongy ground and you needed hard toecaps. Elmer put adverts in the paper and said I was wearing his boots. I suppose I should have asked him to pay me something for the loan of my name, but I never did.

In May we played Huddersfield at Wembley and stayed in a hotel not far away. A beautiful place, nice and quiet. I shared a room with Candy Evans. He came from Pontypool and had played for Halifax. Candy was a second row, about six foot three and fifteen stone ten. He always looked after me. Hell of a lad.

A clean pair of Wembley heels from the Warrington team, 1933.

A greyhound in the slips. Dai is in trap three.

Wembley, 1933. Shankland in possession, Blinkhorn on his right.

Dai shrugs off Fred Brindle at Wembley . . .

. . . and scores. Both Brindle and the Huddersfield winger Ernie Mills (number 2) died in South Africa after emigrating in the 1940s.

I remember at half time at Wembley we were going down the tunnel and there was this loose forward. Brindle his name was, came to Huddersfield from Hull K.R. He was a bloody criminal … terrible fella. I'd scored my first try and Billy Dingsdale had scored his. Brindle ran up to me in the tunnel. 'I'll kill you in the second half', he said. 'I'll twist you in two'. I shouted over to Candy. Boxer, he was. Amateur heavyweight champion of Wales. 'Have you heard this fella, Candy?' I said. 'He's going to kill me second half'. 'I'll

bloody kill him if he does anything to you', said Candy. Brindle left me alone after that. In the second half I scored another brilliant try on the open side from halfway and old man Brindle was nowhere to be seen. I licked him and the fullback. 'Come on', I said to the rest of the lads. 'Only four points to go'.

We didn't make it. We lost the game 21-17. They beat us by two goals but we scored more points on the losing side than any other team that's played at Wembley. I scored two tries that day, from the scrum. I

Dai is introduced to Edward, Prince of Wales, 6 May 1933, at the Huddersfield v Warrington final. On Dai's immediate left are Billy Dingsdale, Nat Bentham and 'Candy' Evans.

really enjoyed myself. I even shook hands with the Prince of Wales. I think he spoke to me more than anyone. Asked me where I came from. 'South Wales', I said. Lance Todd was the commentator on the radio. 'He's still talking to Dai Davies', said Lance Todd. 'He must like the Welsh'. I suppose he did. 'What part of South Wales do you come from?' he said to me. 'Near Swansea', I said. 'Little place called Ammanford'. I couldn't say Garnant. 'I know Ammanford', he said. 'I used to go through it on the train'.

I was the first person from here to play before royalty. When I went to Wembley I had a lot of publicity.[6] I remember a neighbour of mine, Jack Evans his name was. Jack 'Yr Woodland' he was known as and he'd been in America working in the mines. I remember Jack coming back years later and telling me he'd gone to the cinema, the Gaumont Graphic in New York City, and they'd carried the news and pictures from Wembley. There he was in the city of New York and there was I in the city of London, playing for Warrington. When Jack saw me score he told me he jumped up in his seat and started shouting, loud as he could, 'Damn, it's Dai. Damn, it's Dai'. Jack said he couldn't believe it. He started telling everyone who I was and where I came from, until the manager of the Gaumont chucked him out for causing a disturbance.

The best surprise of all was seeing my brother Will before the game. I hadn't seen him for years. Like Jack Evans he'd been travelling. Will must have heard I was playing at Wembley because he came back specially from America. The first thing I knew was when I got this note in the dressing room. It was from Will and he was asking for permission to come in and see me. Will hadn't seen me in fifteen years and there was this note. I couldn't believe it. I was in my football clobber. I wanted to go out but they wouldn't let me because it was too late. Anyway, I told Will to come in and he did. There we were, the players from Warrington wandering about and Will and me hugging each other, just like we were kids.

All my family came up to see me. I was married then and we had our first born. After the game we had a big meal in a pub. I left the team and me and Candy went off with the fellas who'd come from Garnant. There was Archie Rule, a boxer, and his brother, Caradog, from Ammanford. They were living and working in London and had a job on the council. They managed to get us a meal in this pub. There was a party booked in that hadn't turned up and when Archie and Caradog said who we were they gave us the meal without any charge.

Afterwards Will went home with my other two brothers. Me and Candy went back to the hotel in Hendon and Candy looked after me. He was a great pal of mine was Candy. It was a shame what happened to him afterwards. The wife left him and took the daughter and it had a bad effect on him. Candy thought the world of his daughter and losing her in that way broke him up. After he finished playing with Warrington Candy went back to Pontypool and tried to make a go of things on his own. He had a bookmaker's shop and he tried his best but it didn't work out. He was too mixed up. He lost all his money and got depressed and after a bit he gassed himself. He shoved his head in the oven. It was no way to go for a fella like Candy.

I still remember that Wembley weekend. We came back home on the Monday evening. There were big crowds at the station, thousands, and when I came out of the station the crowd surged forward ... like a picket, just like a picket. Bobbies, that's all you could see everywhere, policemen's hats, and the

Members of the Amman Valley Boxing Club, 1925. Tom Evans is seated centre. Archie Rule is seated bottom left.

Training at Wembley. 'Candy' is nearest the camera.

crowd got hold of me and I was lifted up and carried on top of the crowd and into the bus. The top of the bus was open and the crowd were shouting like mad, 'We want Dai-a. We want Dai-a'.[7] From there we went to the town hall and after that to Bob Anderton's pub, The Crown and Sceptre in Warrington. We had to have an escort to get through the town and Candy was alongside me. We landed in Bob Anderton's and the place was packed and they were all jammed in there shouting for me. Mrs. Anderton told me and Candy to go behind the bar and give the lads as much free beer as they wanted. So we went behind. It was the first time in my life I'd pulled a pint of beer but Candy was used to it.

For every one I pulled he was pulling five. The directors of the brewery were there as well, Greenall's Brewery. Candy was asking if they'd give him a pub in Warrington. 'Well, Arthur', they said. 'You've got a pub in Halifax, haven't you?' 'Aye', he said, 'but I play for Warrington now, not Halifax'. The directors turned to me and said, 'What about you, Dai? Would you take a pub?' 'I don't know', I said. 'I will have to see the wife first and talk it over'.

Later on they offered me a pub near the football ground. A nice pub. It was called the Causeway Hotel. But the wife wouldn't take it. She didn't approve of my taking a pub so we pushed it aside.

NOTES

[1] Dai had a high regard for Nat Bentham and remembered him with great affection. Dai often claimed that Nat Bentham was 'the best hooker I ever played with' and that he liked the ball from the scrum half to come at him 'high'. Dai talked often about the visits he and his wife made to Orrell Gardens where the Bentham's lived with their adopted son, Raymond.

[2] Bennett was trainer to Halifax in the 1939 Wembley final.

[3] According to Alan Leigh, curator of Warrington museum, it was felt that Tommy Flynn, although not as exciting a runner with the ball as Jackie Oster, had safer hands and was generally regarded as the steadier player. Legend has it that in the 1933 Wembley final Oster was a nervous wreck. Bill Shankland relates how the team almost had to carry Oster onto the pitch.

[4] Chris Brockbank was the trainer at Huddersfield in 1933.

[5] The River Douglas flows past Central Park.

[6] Dai has also been captured on film by Emyr Evans who, in the 1980s, produced a documentary for S4C on the history of Welsh players in Rugby League.

[7] In Garnant Dai was commonly known as Dai 'Cender'.

5: Caps and Clowns

I wasn't long at Warrington before I got my first cap. I was selected to play for Wales against England at Wigan. It was a midweek match and Billo Rees and I were the half backs. The captain of England was Jonathan Parkin of Wakefield, a good scrum half who was getting on in years. Our hooker was Les White from Pontypridd and I think it was through me that he signed for Hunslet after the game. He had a good match, as regards hooking the ball, and the Hunslet directors approached him. It was me that persuaded Les White to sign.

I played for Wales four or five times but it was during the following season, 1929, that I achieved my greatest honour. The Australians were over here led by Tommy Gorman and they were unbeaten. I'd seen them play the Lancashire side at Warrington and they'd swamped us. They had a helluva team. Wally Prigg was loose forward, Bill Shankland at centre, 'Chimpy' Busch at scrum half and George Treweeke, a tall lad, played second row. In the first test at Hull I was reserve to Billo Rees and they beat us 31-8 at the Boulevard. It was a big disappointment to the rugby league officials. Australia were beating everyone in sight. As a result they decided they had to do something to rescue the tour and they picked a team called the Northern League. 'Pick of the League' we called it, because that's what it was. The very best

Dai, seated second left, in one of his first games for Wales. To the right is Billo Rees.

Glamorgan and Monmouthshire v Australia, 11 December 1929, at Cardiff.

players in the Rugby League. It was a great honour to be selected in that side because there were Australians and New Zealanders playing—they were all eligible. I was picked, along with Jim Sullivan, and we were the only two Welshmen. I think Jim was the captain and Billy Woods was second row and Stanley Smith from Wakefield, he was on one wing, and Lou Brown, the Maori, was on the other. Frank O'Rourke, the Australian, was at centre and Arthur Atkinson from Castleford, I think he was the other centre. Butters from Swinton was at loose forward. Jackie Oster from Wigan—he was playing for Oldham then—he was at half back with me. What a sensation. We beat the Australians 18 to 5. And as for me, I outsmarted 'Chimpy' Busch by a long way.

Jackie Oster and me were picked again for the Northern League. We played the game at St. James's Park, home of Newcastle United.

The Lancashire contingent went the day before and slept up there two nights in a hotel. I remember the ground and the dressing room. We all had boxes with numbers on for our tackle. I could see the tackle box of the great centre forward, Hughie Gallagher of Scotland. It was a marvellous ground. They had lovely dressing rooms and big plunge baths and the physio from Newcastle looked after us. I remember him talking to us after we came off at half time 'What a game', he said, 'Our fellows wouldn't last two minutes of this'.

We lost to the Australians but we played them again at Wembley. I was picked for Wales along with Jess Meredith from Warrington, Billo from Swinton and Tommy Parker. Johnny Ring and Jim Sullivan were selected from Wigan. It was a good game and although we lost 26-10 I felt I did myself justice. I remember the report in The *Daily Express*. It

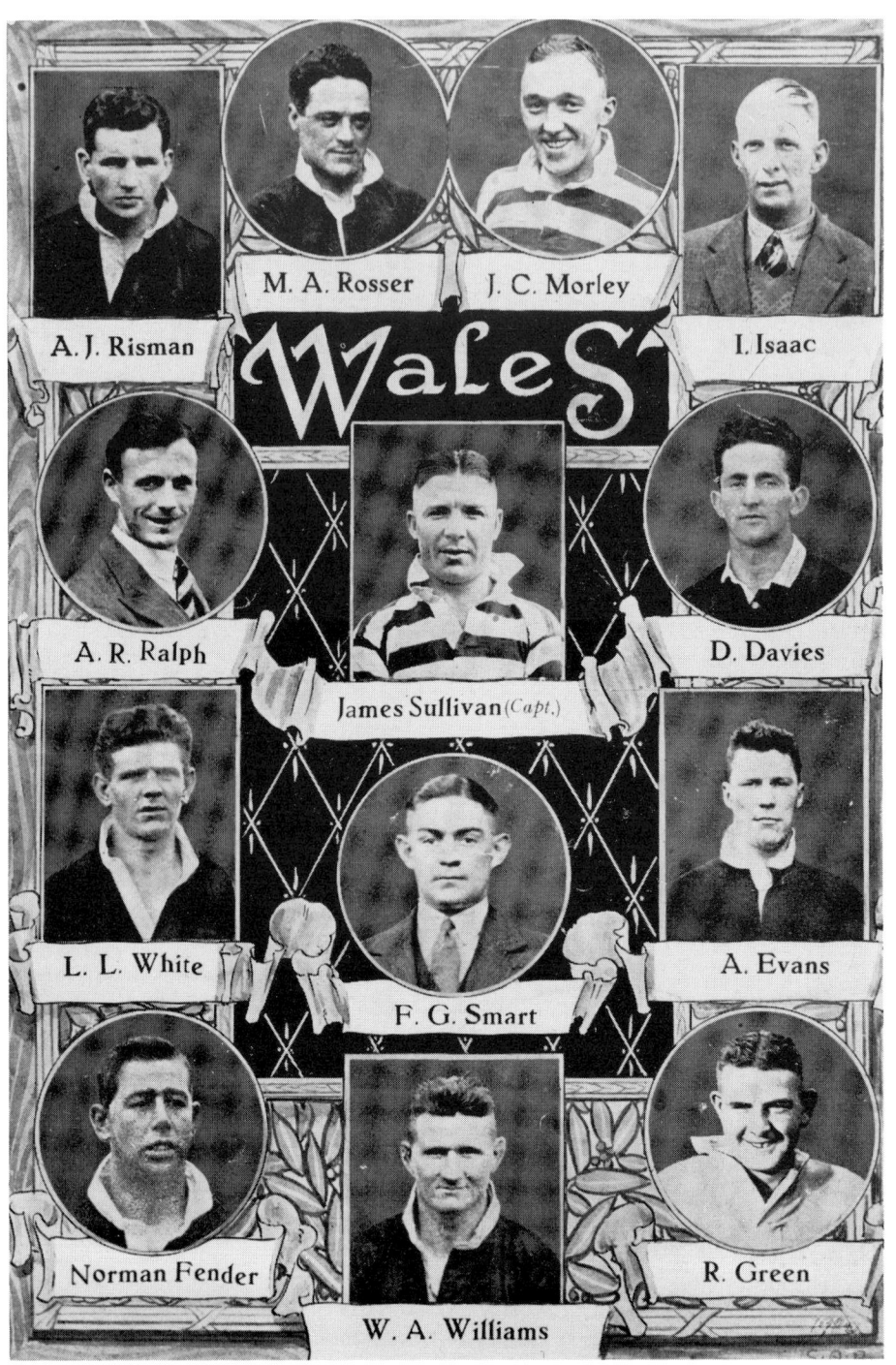

A. J. Risman

M. A. Rosser

J. C. Morley

I. Isaac

Wales

A. R. Ralph

James Sullivan (*Capt.*)

D. Davies

L. L. White

F. G. Smart

A. Evans

Norman Fender

W. A. Williams

R. Green

Wales Rugby League team in the 1930s.

was written by a fellow from Swansea. He used to go to America to cover the fights. Trevor Wignall his name was. I remember the cutting and what it said. 'Although Wales got beaten, one man stood out amongst them. And that was D.M. Davies, the scrum half, who reminded me of the immortal R.M. Owen'. He was referring, of course, to Dicky Owen, the Welsh rugby union scrum half. He played for Swansea and got thirty-five caps for Wales.

A lot happened to me during that season. In April I played against England for the 'Other Nationalities' team up at Halifax. Jim Sullivan was captain and we gave the English a hell of a beating. England were leading 13-0 until I scored a try, full length of the field. In the second half they hardly scored a point and we ended up beating them 35-19. I scored two under the posts. After the second one I joked with Jim. 'I'm making it easy for you', I said, as he came for the kick. Jim and I were very good pals. He always used to ask me before a game, 'How many today, Dai?'

My last game for Wales was in 1935 against France at Bordeaux. I palled with Ossie Griffiths from Pont-rhyd-y-fen, the place where Richard Burton came from. Ossie was loose forward. He went to Wigan and then St. Helens. I'm afraid the Welsh team wasn't up to much on that occasion. The trainers

Stanley Brogden and Stanley Smith in action against Australia in 1932, the tour Dai missed.

told us not to be rough but I think we ended up having three carried off. Three forwards. There were no subs in those days so we played with ten men.

It wasn't a bad trip. We sailed from Folkestone to Calais and travelled by train to Paris. We stayed one night in Paris and went sightseeing for fun around the brothels. On the way home we travelled with Eddie Cantor, the film comedian. On the boat there were lots of flashes and fellas with cameras waiting at Folkestone. We asked what the fuss was about and someone told us Eddie Cantor was going on a trip to England with his daughter. I believe it was his eldest daughter and she acted as his secretary.

As well as France I also went to Ireland. That was in 1934 and I was still with Warrington. The Irish Hospitals Trust, the outfit that ran the lottery in Ireland, invited two teams from the Rugby League to play an exhibition match in Dublin. The Rugby League picked Wigan and Warrington and they took us over to publicise the draw. We travelled from Holyhead to Dublin and stayed in Wynn's Hotel. The food was marvellous. Fresh salmon. The best I ever tasted. I went to see the drum where they made the draw and I pushed my hands into

Other Nationalities v England, 7 April 1930.

53

one of the holes where they pulled out the tickets. We played the exhibition match in Shelbourne Park, the soccer ground, and it was packed out. Wigan beat us 32-19. Hector Gee was playing at scrum half and Charlie Seeling, who'd been transferred to Wigan from Warrington. We had a lad from the Irish Garryowen club, a forward called Griffin. Wigan got a cup and we got horse shoes and replicas of the drum.

They were good years at Warrington. They paid well and I got recognition. I also made a lot of friends. I fell out only once and that was with a fella on the committee, a Tory councillor by the name of Canon Bardsley. He was an arrogant so and so who knew as much about the game of Rugby League as Margaret Thatcher.

My first confrontation with Bardsley was when we played Huddersfield in 1932 at Wembley stadium. So as to avoid any undignified scuffling both teams agreed that the captain of the losing side should keep the ball at the end of the match. At the final whistle I happened to have the ball in my hands and so naturally, I kept hold of it.[2] Bardsley came down from the stand where he was sitting with the Prince of Wales. 'Give the ball here', he said. 'Give me the ball'. I refused but he took the ball off me as I went up the steps for my medal. When I came down I didn't think any more about it.

A few days later I heard Bardsley was displaying the ball in his shop window. He had an off licence and sold wines and whiskies. He'd married late in life and the shop was run

Plotting Wembley the Canon Bardsley way. The players look bemused while Dai keeps his distance.

by two women—his wife and her mother. Anyway, when I heard what Bardsley was up to displaying this ball I decided I'd pay him a visit. I walked in and said, 'Canon Bardsley. Could I please borrow the ball?' 'What for?' said Bardsley. 'Well', I said. 'It stands to reason. I scored two tries with that ball and I wouldn't mind having my photo taken with it. What do you think?' He looked at me and then very reluctantly he gave me the ball. 'Don't forget', he said. 'Bring it back straightaway'.

I took the ball but I didn't give it back. I don't know where it went. Perhaps I gave it to some kids or something. Anyway, the beginning of the following season I bumped into Bardsley as he came out of the committee room under the stand. Everyone went there after the match, including the ladies. There were quite a number of people about when, all of a sudden, I could hear old Bardsley shouting at me at the top of his voice. 'When are you going to bring the ball back, Davies? Don't you remember what I told you?' The tone of his voice annoyed me and when he shouted at me again something flipped inside my head. I grabbed hold of his jacket and pinned him up against the door of the committee room. He started to squeal like a scared rabbit. 'Let go', he yelled. 'This is outrageous'. Bill Roberts, another committee man, came out and shouted at me to let go of Bardsley. 'What's the matter, Billy?' I said smiling. 'There's no damage, is there?' I let go. Bardsley never bothered me after that, not for a long while. I never trusted him though. I always wondered whether he had any hand in my not being picked for the tour of Australia. I suppose that was my biggest disappointment in Rugby League. It was 1932 and I had had two tour trials and played very well. In fact, I'd played perfect football. The day the party was announced the

Warrington supporters couldn't believe I hadn't been picked. No one could. Everyone said there had been skulduggery. I only found out about it later on.[2]

Bob Anderton, the tour manager, never proposed me, or so I was told. Bob was a Warrington committee man and he was on the selection committee for the tour. As luck would have it, Bill Shankland, the captain of Warrington, happened to be in Leeds when they picked the team. Bill spoke to the co-manager, a fella from Oldham called Mr. Hutchins, after they announced the side. 'Isn't Dai playing?' said Bill. 'Isn't Dai picked?' 'No', said Hutchins. 'He wasn't proposed'. 'Whose fault was that?' said Shankland. 'It wasn't mine', said Hutchins. 'It wasn't for me to propose Dai Davies when his own man didn't propose him. And that's the truth'. Bill Shankland never told me. He didn't want to upset me, I suppose. But he came back to Warrington and told Billy Dingsdale. Billy was from St. Helens and he passed the news on to a pal of mine, Jess Meredith, in The Stanley Arms. Jess told me the story later on. 'You can only blame him', said Jess. 'You can only blame Anderton. He didn't want you to go to Australia'. 'Why could that be?' I said. 'I've no idea', said Jess. 'It's probably Canon Bardsley that put him up to it'. I felt disappointed when Jess said that, but he reassured me and told me not to worry. 'Perhaps it's just as well', said Jess. 'You would have been playing the best part of three seasons', he said. 'One after another. Something might have happened and you'd end up a crock. And think of the time you'd be away from your family. Look at it that way'.

So that's what I did. I looked on the bright side. And the fans helped out. That summer they gave a reception for me in the club. They sent a taxi for the wife and gave her a bouquet

Dai's wedding day.

Fifty years later, Dai and Kate celebrate their Golden wedding at Stockton Heath, Warrington, in the company of Jack Hamblet, Dai's great friend.

Dai and Kate at Blackpool.

and presented us both with a Westminster chimer. They put an inscription on it. I still have the clock here in the house.

It took me a long time to get over not being picked. Especially when you consider some of the players they did take—like Jack Feetham the loose forward from Salford, and Ivor Davies, a stand off from Halifax who they put on the wing. It rankled with me. Years after, I talked to Bob Anderton about the tour. He'd been watching Brian Bevan race against a winger from Oldham on Warrington rugby union ground. As Bob was leaving I pulled him up. 'I've got something to ask you', I said. 'You never proposed me for the tour to Australia. You never put my name forward, did you?' He went red. 'You know what I thought of you', he said. 'And what did you think?' 'What do you mean?' he said. 'I think you're telling lies', I said. 'You didn't think much of me when you didn't propose me'. I looked him in the eyes and he walked away.

Bob got picked to go as manager again in 1936. He came back with a boomerang as a souvenir and brought it to the ground. We were all throwing it. I threw it as hard as I could and it broke. Bob was disappointed. I wanted to show him. I wanted him to know I wasn't his plaything.

NOTES

[1] Dai was not the captain of Warrington and should not have kept hold of the ball.

[2] The following remarks are taken from a recorded interview with Kate, Dai's wife, and describe her thoughts on his ommission from the tour side. 'It was an absolute tragedy. He played perfect football in the trials. It was because of our marriage that he didn't get to go. We planned to get married in the summer. That spoiled it for him. That was the reason he was not selected'.

6: Wembley Again

By 1935 I could see there was no future in staying at Warrington and I asked for a transfer. They'd bought some fella from English Rugby Union and they were picking him ahead of me.[2] Although I was on the A team it was part of the contract that they had to pay me four pound a week. My contract was killing them. In any case things weren't going particularly well with Canon Bardsley. So I made the decision: it was time to go.

In 1935 I opted for Huddersfield and I stayed there for almost two years. After the transfer I used to train on Warrington's ground with the Warrington team until Bardsley put a stop to it. After that I trained on my own at the Warrington College ground.

It was strange the first time we played against Warrington. It was at Huddersfield and, naturally, I knew all the chaps.

Warrington were leading 2-0 in the second half when I came up against this ugly-looking forward playing with Warrington called Arkwright. He was a new recruit and he was one of the dirtiest players I ever saw. He'd be out to maim you, hurt you. I had a few words with him on the field and he hit me across the face with a backhander. Soon after there was a scrum on Warrington's line so I thought I ought to teach 'Black Jack' a lesson. Huddersfield won the ball. I picked it up, went for the gap, and passed inside to my loose forward, Aspinall. He scored a try and we won the game. Billy Dingsdale, a pal of mine, saw me afterwards and said, 'Come back with us, Dai. Travel back to Warrington with us on the train'. 'I don't know', I said. 'Who's in charge?' 'I'll go and ask', said Billy and he went away. When he came back I could see

The Huddersfield v Hull Semi-final, 30 March 1935, when the barriers collapsed on the invalid carriages at Headingley.

Huddersfield are introduced to Mr. J. Lewthwaite, Chairman of the Rugby Football League, Wembley, 1935. Accompanying him is Milford Sutcliffe who played professional Rugby League for Huddersfield in 1895 and was captain of the club in 1896.

from his face. It seems he'd spoken to Canon Bardsley. 'He's not coming with us', said Bardsley. 'Why not?' said Billy. 'Because', said Bardsley, 'if it wasn't for him we'd have won the game'.

I'd only been at Huddersfield a few months when we got to Wembley. We played Hull in the semi final at Leeds. There was a hell of a crowd on and they were all swaying. I remember the cripples in their wicker chairs on the touchline and when Mills the right winger scored his tries the crowd jumped up and some of the cripples fell on the deck. You couldn't help but laugh. They made a cartoon of it in the evening paper

It was the last laugh I got for a long while. We played Castleford in the Wembley final and should have won. But for that clown

Tiffany we would have won. Tiffany was one of our second row forwards and he had the ball ten yards from the line. The Castleford centre, Arthur Atkinson—a big, strong-running fella and their star player—came up behind him. I could see he was going to stop our man from scoring and so I shouted to Tiffany to switch it right. 'Give me the bloody ball, Tiffany', I said. 'Give me the bloody ball, you gobbin'. I was the nearest fella to him . . . on his right hand side and if he'd passed it quick I'd have scored under the posts. It was there for the taking, but the bugger held on. He thought he could get there himself, see, but he was easily smothered. That's a second row for you.

It didn't work out for me at Huddersfield. I didn't like the trainer they had. Edgar

Wrigley his name was, a New Zealand white. I never did like the New Zealand whites— give me the Maoris anytime. Wrigley played in that Huddersfield side of 1912 and 1913, the one with Stanley Moorhouse and Albert Rosenfeld on the wings and Johnny Rogers at scrum half. Wrigley never stopped talking about it. Of course, I knew all about Johnny Rogers, seeing as he was Welsh. I met him at his pub, The Plumber's Arms. Johnny used to tell me about the time the players at Huddersfield arranged a race between him and Albert Rosenfeld. There was strong betting on Johnny that he'd beat Rosenfeld but the management of the club stepped in and prevented it from happening. Johnny was one of the best scrum halves to come from down here—he was quick, you know, and built like me. He once scored twenty six tries in a season. People like Wrigley basked in his shadow. And played in it as well. Johnny always said the man was an imposter. That's what I found. Wrigley and me never got on. Many a time he preferred a scrum half who came from Cumberland. Pepperell his name was. In the year after Wembley Huddersfield got to the semi final again but were beaten by Leeds. Old piecan Wrigley had me in the A team that day. The lads at Huddersfield couldn't believe the man's selection. Even Leeds admitted it. 'That's a load off our minds', they said.

Wembley, 1935. Henry Tiffany wades in.

Tommy Scourfield goes down. Dai looks bored.

Edgar Wrigley in his later years at Huddersfield. According to Mick Rhodes, Edgar Wrigley was a genial and good-humoured man.

The brilliant Johnny Rogers. Dai reckoned him one of the greatest of all Welsh scrum halves.

61

BERT WRIGHT'S IMPRESSIONS OF THE STANLEY-KEIGHLEY R.L. CUP-TIE. KEIGH-
ley won by seven points to two.

My next and last Rugby League club was Keighley. It was a homely little place and I thoroughly enjoyed myself. I felt I had a point to prove at Keighley and although I was only there for a season I went to Wembley again for the third time in my career. What a team. Cinderellas, they called us. But we were hardly that. More like geriatrics. Halliday, the hooker, was at least thirty three and the average age of the team was thirty if it was a day.

I remember there was this big factory owner called Booth, a huge chap he was. 'I'm telling you now', he said. 'I'll bet that you'll go all the way to Wembley. I'm not betting you'll win at Wembley', he said, 'but I'll put

Cartoon of the semi-final.

money on you and if you do get to Wembley I'll share it between you'. And he did, reserves and all. Hundred and fifty quid he won for a ten pound stake at 15-1. We shared it out under the stand and had a hotpot supper. It was a fine summer's evening. The club splashed out.

We had a great cup run that year. We even backed ourselves. In the first round we played Hunslet. Jimmy Gill, the loose forward from Leeds—a lad with long arms—came in before the game and gave us the odds. 'Boys', he said. 'I've had six to four given me on this game at Hunslet, so what about it? Shall we put four quid each down?' We all of us threw in the four quid. It was a nice pay day afterwards when we won the game. Six quid back from Jimmy Gill's stake and thirteen pound for winning from Keighley.

In the following round we played home to Broughton Rangers. At one of the scrums Jimmy Gill said to me, 'When you get the ball, Dai, go like hell. The scrum half won't touch you. I'll make sure'. It was our feed so I got the ball and went for it. Jimmy Gill came up from behind and grabbed the opposing scrum half by the pants and held him, so he couldn't bloody move. I kept on going and came to the fullback. It was Bryn Howells, a Welshman from Llansamlet—played a bit of cricket in the Lancashire League. The lad was a slight fella, a left footer, but oh, he had a hell of a kick. He was stood there in front of me—I can see him now—and I wondered what I should do: go round him or try and beat him? Neither. I decided I'd run into him. I knew I was stronger than Howells so I gave it a go. Boom, I flattened him. Trod all over him and under the posts. We won by six points.

Third round we played Liverpool Stanley away from home and we stayed in New Brighton the night before. It was a tight game and a big crowd but we won the game with a try from Fred Talbot, a second row forward who'd come to Keighley from Huddersfield, same as me. We were now in the semi final against Wakefield and we played the game at Leeds. We got a draw out of it but the match itself was terribly dull. A hell of a crowd though, over 40,000. The replay was held at Huddersfield's ground the following Wednesday. We won it in front of a crowd of 15,000 with a try from our halfback, Llewellyn Bevan from Neath. Years later I saw the captain of that Wakefield side, Bill Horton, in a pub he owned in Weston Super Mare. I was on a day trip from Swansea with two pals of mine and we'd come on the steamer. I walked into the pub and there he was, sat behind the bar. 'Don't tell me', he shouted. 'Don't tell me. It's that little swine from

The Wembley line up for Keighley in 1937: D. M. Davies, I. Herbert, R. Lloyd, J. Gill, I. Towill, L. Bevan, G. Parker, J. Sherburn, F. Talbot, C. Halliday, L. Mason, H. Jones, G. Dixon, J. Traill.

Cartoon of the final.

Pontardawe'. 'Almost', I said. We laughed and shook hands and spent the day chatting together in the lounge bar. Bill was a great fella and what with the pub, he'd done well for himself. He asked me how long I'd played up north. 'Thirteen seasons', I said. 'And I got to Wembley in my last game'. 'How did it go?' he said. 'I can't remember'. So I told him. 'We were well beaten'. I said. 'Widnes outdid us. We were a bunch of wandering Welshmen on the day. And they were local —younger than us and all Rugby League'.

I could have carried on playing Rugby League after Wembley but I decided to call it a day. There was a club in Newcastle and they wanted to sign me. Keighley were prepared to let go of me for a hundred and eighty pounds but I didn't go along with it. Maybe I should have done. Keighley would have given me a twenty pound backhander and I could have signed for Newcastle and not bothered turning up. Some would have done it. They'd have taken advantage. Newcastle were a new club and they'd no idea. They found a job for me working in a timber yard but the wife decided she didn't want to move. We'd heard there was a job coming up at Warrington.

NOTES

[1] The scrum half was P.J. Goodall from Blaina who was playing with Nuneaton Rugby Union Club before coming to Warrington. According to Ernie Day, Goodall still lives in Warrington.

Dai getting the ball away following a scrum during the Keighley-Widnes Cup Final.

Happy families in Bronté land.

The after-match Wembley do and what looks like a fun night for the Keighley players!

Dai's Wembley medal, 1937.

Lancashire Combination, winners medal.

Lancashire Cup, winners medal.

Wales Rugby League Cap.

7: The A Train to Amman

The wife it was who spied the advert in the *Warrington Guardian.* The Warrington Junior Rugby League were looking for a coach to work with the amateurs. There were quite a few clubs around Warrington and they played in a league. The advert said they wanted someone to go around the teams on different nights to act as coach. My wife encouraged me to apply for the job and it was she who wrote the letter and made me fill out the application.

There was a short list of three candidates and we had to go in front of a committee at The Crown and Sceptre. I was the last to go up and Bob Anderton of Warrington was on the committee. I explained to him and the committee how I would train the boys. I said it as simply as I could so they would under-

stand. There are three things in rugby, I told them. And once you have mastered them everything else comes easy; passing the ball, left and right, catching the ball, left and right, and kicking the ball. The other important thing is not to kill the youngsters, not to force them along too fast. You must also tell them to watch the good players. If you are playing in a certain position, like scrum half, you must do what I used to do. If there is a midweek match or if you have the chance to study a player on your days off then do it. Practise. Use his methods, try them out and see if they suit. They might not, but at least give them a go like I did. Try new things, that's the secret. It stops you from going stale.

After a while they said, that's alright, Dai,

Dai in an early Pierre Cardin outfit, training the Warrington juniors.

and I went downstairs and had a drink with the other two fellows. There was Tommy Flynn, the stand off half with Warrington, and a forward who played for Widnes— Warrington born, but older than me—toured Australia. We were having our drinks when they came down. Bob Anderton winked and I knew then I'd got the job.

I enjoyed the coaching. I used to go to the Rylands club, the big wire works in Warrington, that's where I did most of my training. It was very enjoyable and I was able to work with some promising players. But sad to say, the job didn't last. In no time at all the war broke out and the job packed up.

The war finished everything. I was working in Thames Board Mills as a blacksmith's striker at the time. The fella who was in the smithy with me had to go to hospital for an operation. They brought another fella in who was twice the blacksmith of the man in hospital. He came from St. Helens, Jackie Parker, and I knew his father. He was the Warrington Rugby League club groundsman when I first went there. Jackie asked me one day, 'How much are you getting, Dai?' I told him. 'Oh', he said, 'You should be getting more than that. You're a semi-skilled man. A blacksmith's striker. You should be on at least two pence an hour more. You're only getting paid the same as a fitter's mate'.

I approached the boss, a Canadian, and he sent me to a fella called Hesse, a short, stiff man—German, I think—and a real tartar. After I'd spoken to him, Hesse called the joiners' mates, fitters' mates and blacksmiths' strikers into his office where he made an announcement. 'I want you to change jobs', he said. 'I want to keep you boys here so you'll not get called up'. There were nine of us in his office and Hesse asked us if we'd all agree to take a different job for less money. The other lads agreed but when it came to me

I refused point blank. 'I'll stay where I am', I said. 'I'm a blacksmith's striker and I'll take a chance on being called up. In my case', I said, 'it means a big drop in wages. I'm a semi-skilled man. If you shift me on to another job I'll lose what's rightfully mine— two pence an hour'.

There was another boss listening to me, a cockney he was, and he looked out of the window as I spoke. 'Why don't you take the job you're offered?' he said. 'Make it easy for yourself'. I turned to him. 'It's nothing to do with you', I said. 'It's none of your business'. I was speaking my mind, of course. I was doing what I always did. But the fellow at the window turned round and showed me the door. He sacked me. On the spot—just for saying a few straight words. Not even a warning, not even a yellow card. They called the security and they walked either side of me, as if I was a criminal, escorted me down to the factory gates.

I felt upset about what happened and it took me a while to get over it. After everything I'd done, after everything that town had meant to me. Naturally I came back home and got a job straightaway in the Gelli Ceidrim. I carried on where I'd left off in 1925.

After the Gelli Ceidrim I went to The Prince Albert pub in Garnant for four years where I built the trade up.[2] I also worked at the ammunition factory down Pembrey and drilled with the Home Guard here in Cwm-aman. After the war ended my wife, Kate, and I went back up to Lancashire. We kept a pub for a while and I joined the training staff at Warrington. I forgot all about the episode at Thames Board Mills and settled back down again with my pals at the club.

In 1952 the wife was getting restless so it was back to South Wales for good. I bought this house in Garnant and for about three

Dai at Thames Board Mills, sensing that the noose is about to tighten.

After the war Dai returned to Warrington as a coach and scout.

The pin-striped coach.

Cwm-gors, the pit Dai hated.

months I went to the Garnant Constitutional Club where the wife and I were steward and stewardess. When that job finished I started work in Cwm-gors colliery.

I didn't like Cwm-gors. It was dangerous. Good money but hard work. Any kind of job was better than Cwm-gors. The boy that took my place in the pit after I left got killed there. Aubrey Rees. Little chap he was. Couldn't speak English very well. Every time I saw him in the pit I used to say to the lads, 'Come on. Start speaking English. Aubrey's coming'. We played tricks on him. The poor fella. Tons of muck fell in and buried him. It was the fault of the managers. They never bothered to shore up the workings. They didn't give a damn. If I'd stayed in Cwm-gors it could have been me.

I did have a few accidents in the pit but that was later on—in the 1950s at the Butcher's colliery, top of Betws mountain, in Ammanford. I was dismantling machinery on the coal face flat on my stomach. The fella I was with put a chain to a steel post and was pulling the machinery. As he was tightening up a stone slid off the lid of the machinery and came on me. I couldn't budge and I started kicking. The fella ran for help and it took five men to slide the stone off me. They got hold of my feet and pulled me out. They couldn't believe I was still breathing. They put me on a stretcher and I was taken to Llanelli hospital in a lot of pain. The doctor injected me in the side and when I winced he said, 'I thought you miners were supposed to be tough'. One of the lads who'd brought me in looked at the doctor. 'You wouldn't talk so blooming fast and you wouldn't talk such damned nonsense if you'd been where he's been'. I came out of it though.

Although I finished playing Rugby League with Keighley I still had some Rugby Union left in me. During the war I played a lot for the Amman. There was a dispensation for Rugby League players so the lads asked me would I turn out for the club. When we started playing I was forty years of age. I hadn't trained or nothing and I was drinking heavy in my own pub, The Prince Albert. The lads insisted and picked me at centre in the Amman first team along with Ted Ward. I didn't do too bad I suppose. I was out of breath, you know, and I wasn't as fast but I still had the knack of timing a run. They kept picking me at centre and they would have picked me in my old position at scrum half but Ted Ward's father butted in and said I was too old. Ted, of course, was younger than me. He signed for Wigan before the war but there were no jobs in Wigan so he came back here. If he hadn't come back he'd have been called up. Ted worked in the colliery same as me. Labouring. It was hard graft in the pit.

The first game we played was against Tumble and there was a heck of a crowd watching. Tumble had a player—a huge lad —Handel Greville. This Greville had an international cap and a big crowd came to watch him play but, *Duw,* I moth-eat the fella —I danced all over him. Afterwards, I felt a bit sorry. The crowd had come to watch him not me, and yet he couldn't control me.

Ted Ward, Amman, Llanelli and Wigan.

After that I got picked for West Wales; Dai Bevan's team it was called and I was captain. We played the Air Force and the proceeds went to the Amman Valley Cottage Hospital. Willie Davies was playing stand off for the Air Force and Haydn Tanner was reserve scrum half. The crowd came to watch Willie but he broke no eggs. From what I could see he wasn't as good as Billo Rees. He didn't have his speed. Billo was very deceiving in his speed.

I did well against the Air Force and scored a try from forty yards out. I beat the fullback, a lad named Wyndham Lewis—he's dead and buried now. Wyndham Lewis had just signed for Wigan. He was supposed to take Jim Sullivan's place. What a hope! After a bit Wigan gave him away on a free to Hull K.R. Lewis was from Ammanford and worked in the same colliery as me but he was a bad'un. He left the mines and became a policeman. He used to catch fellows on the beat and ask them for a bribe. They say he used to knock his wife about as well. The day he faced us he banged no one up. He played the game like Mr. Plod. I walked straight over him from forty yards.

We had a strong team that day and I was allowed to play scrum half. We were all Rugby League. Ted Ward was in the centre—he was

Back Row, left to right: Dai, Billo Rees, Ike Fowler. Front Row: Ted Ward, Arthur Price, Evan Phillips, Emrys Evans.

only twenty two—and Gwyn Parker from Aberavon was the other centre. Gwyn had been with Huddersfield and was a lot younger than me. Edgar Morgan from Ammanford was in the side as well and he was with Hull.[2] We were a bit too clever for the Air Force. A lot of our lads had played Rugby League and the Air Force's hadn't. There was plenty of space. That's the difference between the games. There are far more gaps in Rugby Union. It's only when you play Rugby League, when you play something different, that you see where the space is. Two fellas more in Rugby Union, yet the gaps are wider.

NOTES

[1] David Evans of Brynaman, a noted photographer and lifelong acquaintance of Dai Davies, tells us how Dai used to do party tricks for the customers in The Prince Albert. One of these involved putting his hand on the counter of the bar and jumping from one side to the other from a standing position. Dai loved to prove how agile he was.

[2] One of the few occasions where Dai is mistaken. The other centre to Ted was Douglas Bowen of Ammanford and York. And according to the report in the *Amman Valley Chronicle,* of 20 February 1941, Edgar Morgan did not play. The trainer of the Air Force team was Albert Jenkins.

8: The First and the Last

In my opinion the start of the Rugby League was the James Brothers of Swansea. I know more about the James Brothers than anybody because I played for the same club, Broughton Rangers, and there were pictures of Sammy and Billy in the dressing rooms and the committee rooms. They called them the curly haired marmosets and they won the cup for Broughton when they beat Salford in 1902. I don't know where they played but it wasn't at Wembley.

There were five brothers—Dai and Evan played for Swansea and Wales. The next two were Sammy and Billy. Sammy was a scrum half and Billy was a stand off. Then there was another brother, Claude. I don't know whether it's true or not, but they used to say how the lads would go in the pantry at tea time and pass out the jam, the cups and saucers and the loaves of bread like they were handling rugby balls, while another fella caught them and stacked the table.

The whole family went north and then, after a while, they came back home and were reinstated. It's only been done once I think.

Willie and Claude James.

They were reinstated and after that they went north again.

Sammy and Billy had a big reputation up north. Not that it did them much good. Sammy was always in poor health and he died young. Billy was a tippler. The old fellas said they had to go hunting for Billy before a game. They never knew whether they'd find him in the pub or not. That's what they told me at Broughton Rangers. Maybe it was true—you wouldn't know for sure.

I remember once playing in a trial at Broughton and there was a building contractor there by the name of Kennedy. A committee man and Chairman of the Rugby League he was, typical dim wit. Broughton had these trials at the beginning of the season, every club did it, and they used to bring players in to see if they could find anyone better. This one day Kennedy comes up to me and he says, 'You're playing for your place next Saturday, Dai. You'll have to be a flier'. 'Oh', I said, 'and why is that?' 'We've got Sammy James coming up', he said. 'And if he's half as good as his father was, I'm telling you now, you've got something on'. 'Who's Sammy James?' I said. 'You'll find out', he said. So they tried him out. But pooh, I moth-eat the lad. He wasn't in the same street as his father. He'd come up for the day from the Rugby Union and he didn't even know where he was, never mind the rules. The pressure got to him. I suppose it was hard.

At times, fellas like Kennedy talked a lot of rubbish. He might have built big houses but he wasn't too good at looking after rugby players. 'We made you', he said to me when I asked for a transfer. 'We made you'. Fancy saying that to a professional footballer—and him the Chairman of the Rugby League. 'You never made me', I said. 'I made myself'. Of course I did. To be good at something—boxing, football—whatever it is, you've got to be born with it. It has to be in you somehow. Jackie Hamblett told me that at Warrington. And Jackie had seen a lot of Rugby League. He was the baggage and kit man at the Warrington club for over fifty years.

You can't coach talent. It's either in you or it isn't. I remember a conversation I once had with Billy Woods at Wigan when Ted Ward was coach. It was back in the fifties and we were living in Garnant. We'd decided to go to Blackpool for the Illuminations—me, the wife, Jim 'Y' Gass, Roy James and Freddie Davies. We went by car and called in at

Dai's life-long friend Jack Hamblet in the Warrington boot room.

Wigan to see how Ted was doing. His landlady was a Welsh woman called Mrs. Toy—she married an Irishman—and she told me that Ted was down at the ground. I walked down and met Billy Woods. Billy and me played for Warrington and Billy was managing The Royal Oak at the time, the pub near the ground, the one Johnny Thomas had. We went to the club and Billy introduced me to a few of the directors. They all knew who I was. I'd played there so many times.

We'd watched Ted trying to coach this big, hulking forward and Billy said to me, 'Do you believe in coaching, Dai?' I looked at what Ted was trying to do. 'Not like that', I said. 'In any case, how do you coach someone who's not in your own position? How is a forward going to coach me?' I said. 'Me, a scrum half. What's he going to say to me?' 'I quite agree with you', said Billy Woods. 'Look at that team of Swinton's', I said, 'when Billo was there. They had a trainer, a good trainer. But as for ability, they introduced it, like Billo Rees. You can't coach ability. There are only three things you can coach in a lad', I said. 'How to catch a ball, how to kick a ball and how to pass a ball. Everything else should be natural for you. You can't tell a fella how to run', I said. 'It's either in you to sidestep or it isn't. You know what I mean? Sometimes you see a fella try a sidestep and look what happens, his legs get tangled and down he goes'.

The directors were there, including Tom Brown, the Chairman of the club. Tom was landlord of The Park Hotel. There were also two brothers. One used to play for Oldham. I played against him, and he was a good scrum half. The other had a big window cleaning business in Wigan. While we were chatting I said to them, 'What would you give for another Jim Sullivan?' They looked at me and smiled. 'Twenty thousand pounds', said

A classic shot of Sullivan toward the end of his career.

Tom Brown. 'And we'd give twelve for you, Dai'. Those were his very words. 'Twelve thousand'. I think that shows what they thought of me in Wigan.

When I was at Warrington there were a pile of Welsh players. There was Jess Meredith from Ebbw Vale. He'd played for Abertillery and signed on with Les Perkins. Jess was a big fella, fifteen stone. They changed him from a centre to a second row forward—that's fairly typical in rugby league and tells you something about the difference in pace. Jess could do it because he was a good tackler. I remember in 1928, before he moved to second row, we were playing Huddersfield in the third round of the cup. They had two centres, both Aussies, and one of them was a tall, lanky bugger. First scrum, they passed

the ball out and this fella took it. Jess was opposite him and bang, he hit him with everything he had. The Aussie was jiggered and never came right. They took him off after that and we won the game. From there on Jess always played second row.

The only thing Jess was funny about was his name. Jess Oswald Meredith he was called but he didn't like anyone calling him that. 'Don't call me Jess', he used to say. 'Call me Kikey'. 'Why Kikey?' I said. 'I don't know', said Jess. 'Just call me Kikey, that's all'. Jess was like that. He came from Ebbw Vale and couldn't speak Welsh. The thing is, he liked the other players to think he was fluent. Jess used strange words no one could understand. A lot of strange words. It was all gibberish and he made it up so players would think he was speaking in Welsh. I don't know why he did it. Maybe he wanted the lads to think he knew things they didn't. Maybe that was the reason. After he retired Jess became a bookie and a few years later he died of cancer. He was buried in the crematorium in Warrington. A few of his pals from Ebbw Vale were at the funeral.

A lot of rugby players went north from round here. I remember the boy from Gwauncaegurwen, Emrys Evans. They called him Enoch. What a lad he was. By God, he could gallop. He once challenged Ted Ward to a race round the streets in Garnant. Ted always bragged he could beat him for pace when Salford played Wigan. 'That was Wigan, not Garnant', yelled Enoch, and away he galloped. Completely ran away with it. Left Ted for dead.

Ted was a centre at Llanelli and Wigan, but in my opinion he wasn't that quick.[1] And I doubt he was as skilful as Tommy Parker from Aberavon. Tommy went to Wigan and Gwyn, his brother, was signed by Huddersfield. Both were good centres. I believe Gwyn

Tommy Parker.

is alive yet, but Tom isn't, he's dead and buried. Tom spent a lot of time in France after he left Wigan. Then he came back here and married a widow in a place called Cwm Afan—where that actor came from, Richard Burton. My brother Will knew Burton's father. Drank in a pub near Pont-rhyd-y-fen near to Cwm Afan—little fella he was with snow-white hair.

My stand off half, Eddie Williams, at Neath, he went north. Eddie was from Cwmllynfell. A good little fella he was. He had a couple of caps. He played New Zealand in 1924 and France in 1925, then went to Huddersfield. He was around the same time as Eddie Watkins, the scrum half. Eddie Watkins was at Cardiff and went to Halifax. I played against Eddie Williams and Eddie Watkins, up north. They were both internationals but I could lick them easy. Especially Eddie Watkins. He was only a little fella and, duw, I could flatten him. I was taller than him and he seemed to be frightened … you could sense it almost. Eddie didn't last long in Halifax, then he came home. I suppose he packed up about the same time as Jack Elwyn Evans.

Jack played with me at Broughton, like I told you earlier, and after he retired he kept the Bridgend pub in Brynaman. Jack was a lot older, but boy was he tough. He was in the First World War and got wounded in the shoulder—had shrapnel in it. Jack Elwyn was good with his dukes. I remember they had this winger at Broughton who came from Swinton. When Jack arrived he took his place. One night after training, this winger came up and threatened Jack in the dressing room. Well, by God, you should have seen what happened. Jack knocked hell out of him. He gave this fella a belt in the chops and sent him flying right across the room, out through the door.

Eddie Watkins, one of Dai's half-back contemporaries who never settled in Rugby League.

79

Jack Elwyn Evans signed for Broughton along with Evan Phillips. Both were products of Amman United.

Another like him who was good with his mitts was Jerry Shea from Newport. Now Jerry was a real footballer, big fella with a sidestep. He was also a middleweight professional boxer and he played for Wigan in the 1920s when they had the makings of that great team. Me and Jerry were pals.

We had the pick of the bunch up north in those days, except for one or two. There were always some who didn't take the ticket and who should have done, like Dan Jones at Neath. Dan was capped by Wales and still holds the record of tries in a season, seventy two I believe it is. Dan was offered a chance to go north but he said, 'I'm too old. I wouldn't like to take their money'.[2] Dan could sidestep and he could run. Another fella held the record in Wales before him and he played for Warrington as well, Billy Rhodes. Billy had the record when he played for Pontypridd. Some achievement for a man who lost a finger during World War One.

My predecessor from Garnant was Billo Rees. He went to Swinton around 1923. When he first went north Billo couldn't get his place. He came back here for a bit and worked in the colliery. He had to hang around until a fellow called Bert Jenkins from Pen-y-graig in the Rhondda packed in at Swinton. When Billo returned to Swinton he was outstanding and made the grade in no time. Swinton were silly—unbelievable really—in depriving Billo of first team football. A player with his talent. There were few stand off halves with Billo's ability. Not during my time. I mean, there were people like Gwyn Richards who got his cap with Cardiff and went off to Huddersfield. But it was chalk and cheese comparing Gwyn Richards with Billo Rees. In his own position Billo was the best. There's never been better. For his signing on fee he got what I got—three hundred and fifty, same as Ted Ward.

In 1928 Billo was picked to go on tour to Australia. But he had a bad time of it. He ended up playing scrum half in Australia

Three all-time greats from Wales. Jim Sullivan, Jerry Shea and Johnny Ring, all played for Wigan in the 1920s.

because Bryn Evans, his own cell mate from Swinton, was having a bad tour. Billo told me that afterwards. There were the two Evanses at Swinton, Bryn and Jack. They both went on tour in 1928 and 1932 as well. In 1932 Bryn Evans was selected ahead of me. Bryn, Jack and the older brother, 'Chick', they were all born in Swinton. Their father had lived in Garnant and was in the tin works here and went north for a job. I'd safely say that Bryn Evans was the slowest scrum half that every played rugby. How he got himself picked to go to Australia is completely beyond me. Some say he was a freemason… you wouldn't know. In 1928 him and Jonathan Parkin were selected to play scrum half.

Parkin, the captain, was from Wakefield, and during the tour he broke his thumb and so he was out. Bryn Evans didn't come up to expectations and they put Billo at scrum half with Leslie Fairclough as the other stand off. Billo should never have agreed to play scrum half. I remember him from Amman United and when he played for Llanelli. He was always a stand off. I will admit that when he first went to Llanelli Billo had to play scrum half for a bit until the regular stand off—W.J. Davies—was transferred to Hull. But that didn't last.

They talk about the standard of Rugby Union in those days but most of the lads who made the grade ended up going north. A few

British Tourists 1928. Back Row: N. Bentham, A. Ellaby, H. Bowman, J. Thompson, C. Dolan, H. Williams, J. W. Brough. Third Row: J. Evans, R. Sloman, H. Young, A. E. Fildes, W. Burgess, W. Houghton, J. Sullivan, H. Halfpenny. Second Row: W. Bowden, J. Oliver, A. Frodsham, G. F. Hutchins, J. Parkin, E. Osborne, T. E. Gwynne, W. Bowers, M. Rosser. Front Row: B. Evans, L. Fairclough, D. Murray (trainer), T. Askin, W. Rees.

Broughton 'A team', 19 November 1927, four days after Dai signed for Warrington. Dai's friend, Bill Wootton, is captain.

missed out like Albert Jenkins, a centre and one of the big sensations in Welsh rugby. He had fourteen caps and yet somehow he slipped through the net. When I went to Broughton they had an old forward from Pontypool called Bill Wootton. Bill had a bald head and played with pads on his knees but he was a great forward and he could handle the ball. Bill Wootton told me he was once given a thousand pound cheque to sign Albert Jenkins. Bill said he travelled down here to sign him on but when he got to Llanelli he had to be wary in his conversation. Bill asked where it was best to get hold of Albert and the fellas he talked to said there was only one place for Albert and that was The Salutation in Llanelli. Bill had a photograph of Albert Jenkins in his pocket and when he walked in he could see Albert in a bad way tumbling it back. Bill was shocked. 'I couldn't do it', he said. 'I couldn't give him the money. He was in cloud cuckoo land. In any case', he said, 'drunk or sober, I'd rather have had another thousand pound in my pocket and found Tommy Howley'.

Bill was meaning Tommy Howley of Ebbw Vale. Tommy never had a cap down here but he went to Wigan in the early twenties, the time of Johnny Ring, and Bill had played against him at Broughton. Tommy was a centre and went on tour in 1924. He wasn't a big chap but Bill always said there was no comparison between him and Albert Jenkins. That was Bill's version anyway. He didn't approve of the way Albert Jenkins conducted himself in The Salutation. Mind you, there were plenty in Wigan who didn't approve of Tommy Howley's behaviour. When I was up north there were stories flying here and there about how Tommy Howley put women in

Tommy Howley of Ebbw Vale, who formed a marvellous partnership with Johnny Ring at Wigan.

Albert Jenkins of Llanelli and Wales.

Wigan in the family way. Who's to say different? Lads don't always behave, I suppose. It's a great temptation when you're young and famous and the women are watching your every move.

Another great centre of that period was Danny Hurcombe, the lad from Tal-y-wain. Jim Sullivan always said Danny Hurcombe was the 'complete footballer' and could play anywhere, like Billy Boston. When I saw Danny he was getting on, but on his day he was still brilliant. Jim told a lot of stories about Danny. He said Danny was a heavy smoker and never went anywhere without his dog, Bess. He even took Bess in the changing rooms before a game, said Jim, and once he got changed he'd light up his pipe. Jim said the smoke was that thick sometimes they had to tell Danny to go and stand outside. According to Jim it was not a very professional atmosphere. The dog would start barking and half the team'd be choking to death.

Danny Hurcombe from Tal-y-waun, a brilliant all-rounder from the early 1920s.

Sid Jerram and George 'Dodger' Owens played together for Swansea and were signed by Wigan for £180 each in 1913. They formed one of the club's finest half-back combinations.

Danny was in the same team as Sid Jerram and Dodger Owens, a great pair of halfbacks. They played with Jim Sullivan in the great Wigan side of the 1920s, the one that included Johnny Ring and Jerry Shea, and the South African pair Van Heerden and Van Rooyen. Sid and Dodger came from Swansea and played a bit before me, although I do have a recollection of watching Sid Jerram after he'd gone to Wigan Highfield at the back end of his career. Sid and Dodger signed before the First World War for two-hundred pounds a piece, a big sum of money in those days when you consider what a fella's weekly wage was.

Later on I used to meet Dodger regularly in Swansea. He carried this picture of Billy Trew in his football clobber. He always showed you this picture of Billy Trew, whether you wanted to see it or not, but he never let you catch hold of it. You understand me? Dodger was afraid someone might steal it. 'The best player that ever lived', Dodger would say. 'The one and only W.J. Trew. The finest footballer Wales produced'. Billy Trew played for Swansea at centre and stand off before the war years and got his first cap on the wing. He didn't go north although his son did, Billy Junior. He went to Swinton to take Billo Rees's place but never made the grade. A nice fella all the same, though. Billy Trew, the son, lived in Swansea somewhere and he had a pub and at times I used to call in to see him and Dodger. It was always, 'Hallo, D.M. How are things with you?' Then he'd serve me a drink. I never spent a penny inside Billy's pub. He was a gentleman. I'm not so sure you'd say the same thing about the old man. It struck me old Trew was something of a big head. Like that Q.C. fella who played for Swansea, Judge Rowe Harding. It's a pity the pair of them never went north, they'd have had it knocked out of them.

I remember W.J. Trew as a referee on this ground down here: Amman United. I was in school in Glanaman at the time and the Amman were playing in the Welsh Cup. The Amman had knocked Ystalyfera, Resolven and Skewen out in the earlier rounds and this was the semi final. I was about nine or ten years old at the time and all the kids were packed in, heck of a crowd, and all going mad, of course.

Joe Rees was playing for the Amman that day. Damn, he was good. He wasn't big but he used to train all the time. Hardy fella. Kick with either foot and a heck of a tackler. Anyway, one of the Aberavon players got hold of the ball, a fella named Jim Jones I think it was, Welsh international forward. I swear to God he was yards off side when he got the ball but Trew ignored it. We all knew why. Amman had already beaten Swansea and Swansea was Trew's old club. Of course, he didn't like the idea of Amman United, a second-class team, upsetting the form book and beating a first-class team like Aberavon. That's my opinion. This Jones was a huge fella, over six foot tall and sixteen stone and

Amman United, 1914-15 and the team that played Aberavon in the controversial semi-final of the Welsh Hospitals Cup. Garfield Phillips is seated first left, second row up. Joe Rees, fourth left, same row.

Charlie Seeling, top row, fourth from left in the first of the great Wigan sides, 1910.

Eleven of Warrington's half backs are captured together at Wilderpool stadium on Monday, 8 December 1969. Top row, left to right: Bill Aspinall, Parry Gordon, Bobby Fulton, Warren Ayres, Peter Harvey. Front row, left to right: Dai Davies, Tommy Flynn, Jack Goodall, Ron Ryder, Jackie Edwards, Jackie Fleming.

Dai, at home, in the last year of his life.

when he got the ball he crossed over Joe Rees's tackle and Trew gave a try. Aberavon won the game, three points to nil.

It was a big disappointment but Trew was above it. He walked round the park like he was up on a pedestal. A big head, you know. Not in the same street as the lad from Broughton, Albert Harding. With Albert reffing there was always give and take. A bit of scope, as they say.[3]

Mind you, rugby is all about controversy. That's the fun of it. A sport with no argument isn't worth the bother. That came home to me the time I met the one and only Charlie Seeling. Charlie was a member of the All Blacks side of 1905, the one beaten by Wales with that controversial try from Dr. Teddy Morgan. Charlie Seeling played in that match and it was always my ambition, if I could, to meet him, if only because Dr. Teddy Morgan's family lived near Garnant.

After the 1905 tour Charlie went back to New Zealand if you remember, where he buried his wife. There was only him and his son—young Charlie—left, so he came over to England and signed for Wigan. Charlie was a great forward, hell of a tackler and very determined. At the time I played his son was with Warrington. Charlie senior kept a pub in Wigan. The Roebuck Hotel. I'd never met the old man so one day at Warrington I said to young Charlie, 'Why don't you bring your father to a match? I've heard such a lot about him. Tell him they think the world of him in Wales'. Charlie and I were good pals and so he told his father what I said and the following week he brought him in the dressing room before the game. I shook hands with him. *Duw, Duw,* his fist was like a ham bone. It collared mine … smothered it. 'I know what you're going to ask me', he said straightaway. 'It's about the try Teddy Morgan scored'. 'That's right', I said. 'You must agree Wales

were a good team in those days. Gwyn Nicholls, the centre, and Willie Llewellyn from Llwynypia on the wing. And then there was the Dancing Dicks', Owen and Jones, at half back'. Charlie nodded. 'But I'll tell you one thing', he said. 'If Dr. Teddy Morgan scored that try … if he scored that try in 1905 so did our man Deans score his try too. And it was a fairer try than Morgan's. Deans was tackled by one of the centres but he was over the line and the try was disallowed. The referee said he was on his back. But I'm telling you it was a fair try. Nine times out of ten today they'd give that try. And as for Morgan, he was well into touch. I know it because I was the nearest New Zealander to him'.

Charlie was still remembering the story as they called the teams together for the match. As I left the dressing rooms we shook hands and Charlie patted me on the back. That was a great thrill for me. People in Wales still talked about Charlie. Even my father. Charlie was in at the start, you see. He remembered a lot about the great old players.

I was lucky to go north, especially when I did. Whatever's happened since I retired, I doubt the standards have got any better. Players today are fitter, I suppose, but whether they're as crafty, I doubt it. You only have to look at the talent there was when I went north. Jim Sullivan and Billo Rees, Jonathan Parkin and Johnny Ring, Jackie Oster and Tommy Flynn, Tiny Van Rooyen and Stanley Smith. I got the chance to see players. In my time at Warrington I played against people from all over the world: Van Heerden from South Africa, Bill Shankland from Australia, Lou Brown from New Zealand. In the '20s and '30s they were all coming in. You don't get to see much better than that. And after it was over I didn't lose touch either. None of us did. The fellas that watched and the friends we made never forgot us. That was important. That was the main thing. They kept in touch wherever we got to later on.

A few years ago Warrington gave a reception for me. Alex Murphy was there and he gave a speech and said what I'd done. Alex Murphy, now there's a footballer for you—him and Andy Gregory from Wigan. It's only a pity they didn't kick a ball when I was around. Of course I'd have moth-eat 'em.

This letter from Bill Shankland, written almost sixty years after they played together, shows something of the respect in which Dai was held.

> No 1 FLAT, 2 St Clair Rd,
> Canford Cliffs, Poole,
> Dorset. BH13 7JR.
> 2.2.90.
>
> Dear Dai,
> I was pleased to hear from Ennis Day of Warrington that you are now in your home Country, and living with your son.
> I've often spoken about you and wondered where you got to.
> You were one of the greatest ½ backs I ever played with, and I often think we were born 40 years too soon. However, although the last year or so has been dificult because my dear wife had a stroke, I none the less say to her we are luckier than plenty. It's no good crying.
> I have 2 sons in America + one in London, all doing well for themselves, thank God.
> If ever I am in your area I'll certainly look you up.
> In the meantime God Bless and Daph & I send our best wishes to you & yours,
> Sincerely,
> Bill Shankland

NOTES

[1] The relationship between Dai and Ted Ward was full of rivalry and banter. Sometimes they sat with their own groups of 'supporters' at opposite sides of the Garnant Constitutional Club and bragged about the past and who had done what. From what I can gather this went on for years. Dai told many stories about the bets that were placed when brother Will hit town and challenged the Ward family as to who had the better career, Ted or Dai.

[2] Dan Jones scored 59 tries for Neath in 1928-9.

[3] According to the *Amman Valley Chronicle* 'Some partisans of the home team seem rather disappointed with the way Mr. Trew officiated. Let me say here at once that I thought him an ideal referee'. 'Old Sport' The *Amman Valley Chronicle,* 21 April 1914.

Playing Record

Compiled by Robert Gate

BROUGHTON RANGERS

Debut 30.1.1926 v Widnes (H), lost 3-5

	A	T	G	P
1925-26	15	—	—	—
1926-27	34	6	—	18
1927-28	6	—	—	—
TOTALS	55	6	—	18

Last game 12.11.1927 v Wigan (H), won 10-8

WARRINGTON

Debut 26.11.1927 v Wigan Highfield (A), lost 5-11

	A	T	G	P
1927-28	20	3	—	9
1928-29	4	—	—	—
1929-30	33	4	—	12
1930-31	17	—	—	—
1931-32	39	9	—	27
1932-33	37	10	—	30
1933-34	36	7	—	21
1934-35	10	1	—	3
TOTALS	196	34	—	102

Last game 3.11.1934 v Keighley (A), lost 10-13

HUDDERSFIELD

Debut 2.2.1935 v Dewsbury (A), lost 5-11

	A	T	G	P
1934-35	15	1	—	3
1935-36	18	1	2	7
TOTALS	33	2	2	10

Last game 29.4.1936 v Featherstone Rovers (A), won 20-13

KEIGHLEY

Debut 29.8.1936 v Wakefield Trinity (H), lost 11-25

	A	T	G	P
1936-37	35	12	1	38

Last game 8.5.1937 v Widnes (Wembley), lost 5-18

CAREER RECORD

	A	T	G	P
Broughton R	55	6	—	18
Warrington	196	34	—	102
Huddersfield	33	2	2	10
Keighley	35	12	1	38
Wales	4	—	—	—
Other Nats	1	2	—	6
Glamorgan and Monmouthshire	5	—	—	—
Glamorgan v Monmouthshire	1	—	—	—
Tour Trials 1932	2	—	—	—
Rugby League XIII	3	—	—	—
Grand Totals	335	56	3	174

INTERNATIONAL APPEARANCES

11.1.1928
Wales 12 England 20 at Wigan
18.1.1930
Wales 10 Australia 26 at Wembley
7.4.1930
Other Nats 35 England 19 at Halifax (2 tries)
30.12.1933
Wales 19 Australia 51 at Wembley
1.1.1935
Wales 11 France 18 at Bordeaux

4.12.1929
Rugby League XIII 18 Australians 5 at Wigan
18.12.1929
Rugby League XIII 22 Australians 32 at Newcastle
17.3.1934
Rugby League XIII 32 France 16 at Warrington

COUNTY APPEARANCES

11.12.1929
Glam & Mon 9 Australians 39 at Cardiff
21.12.1929
Glam & Mon 6 Cumberland 14 at Cardiff
27.2.1930

Glam & Mon 13 Yorkshire 6 at Hunslet
12.4.1930
Glam & Mon 3 Lancashire 29 at Warrington
21.3.1931
Glam & Mon 19 Cumberland 12 at Whitehaven

30.4.1927
Glamorgan 18 Monmouth 14 at Pontypridd

TOUR TRIALS
10.2.1932
Reds 3 Whites 22 at Warrington
9.3.1932
Whites 7 Reds 10 at Leeds

CHALLENGE CUP FINAL
14.4.1928
Warrington 3 Swinton 5 at Wigan
6.5.1933
Warrington 17 Huddersfield 21 at Wembley (2 tries)
4.5.1935
Huddersfield 8 Castleford 11 at Wembley
8.5.1937
Keighley 5 Widnes 18 at Wembley

LANCASHIRE CUP FINAL APPEARANCE
19.11.1932
Warrington 10 St. Helens 9 at Wigan (try)

Surfing the Hurricane

Phil Melling

Those who see themselves as victims, Robert Hughes argues, do not profess a common humanity or a shared dignity but authenticate what they say by their membership of an interest group. In the world of the victim, says Hughes, there is no such thing as a disinterested, universal language of culture. The impersonal viewpoint does not exist. Gay people are allowed to talk about gay issues but heterosexuals are not; men cannot talk about women; whites cannot talk about blacks. To speak for others is considered inauthentic. The victim can only speak for himself.[1]

A further critique of the victim is provided by Geoffrey Moorhouse in an excellent collection of articles entitled *At the George and other Essays*. In a concluding piece Moorhouse discusses the appeal of Queensland's Wally Lewis and examines, in detail, Lewis' behaviour in front of a large, partisan crowd at Lang Park, Brisbane. At one point Lewis is hit off the ball and falls to the ground in a theatrical manner, his arms stretched out in the shape of a cross. The crowd reacts aggresively. 'Christ', yells a fan, 'our Wally's been "crucified"'. Moorhouse interprets the significance of the gesture and Lewis' style in the following terms: 'He is an outstanding athlete ... His has been a tremendous success story, with much well-deserved applause. And yet he... obviously has a deep psychological need to see himself as a victim, even when he's winning. That I don't understand at all'.[2]

Moorhouse situates Lewis in the context of an unparalleled career in club, State of Origin and Australian Rugby League Football. The genius of Lewis is unquestionable, he argues, but the talent is flawed and the stature of the man undermined by a chronic tendency toward 'pubescent mateship'. A play-acting manner ill befits Lewis' considerable talents and the awards and accolades the game has bestowed upon him. The role is calculating yet enigmatic, says Moorhouse; Lewis conveys a glancing empathy with the fans in the bleachers yet he does it in the knowledge that the lives of the fans are far less privileged than his and that their wider grievances about the political bias and chauvinism of Sydney or Canberra are not without some historical validity. Rugby League, says Moorhouse, has no need to cultivate an image of 'superstardom and glitzy success'. Nor should it play to the needs of the gallery. The game must abandon the trappings of victimisation, for this is simply a 'confidence trick perpetrated upon the viewer'. In its purest form it must seek to represent the natural restraint and grace under pressure that is best typified in the north of England in towns like Wigan and in the more traditional activities of miners, mill workers and British Rugby League players.[3]

If you come from Wigan, as I do, and if you are born and brought up, as I was, within spitting distance of Central Park, the son of a miner who spent his life watching Rugby League, your instincts point you in the same direction. There is a dignity that silences even the most vocal opposition among those who take their adversity on the chin, and who, at times of crisis, do not indulge in extravagant gestures or needless self pity. Such was the case with my own father who lost an eye in a mining accident and suffered greatly with pleurisy and pneumoconiosis after he left the pit. His predicament was not uncommon nor was his strange and bitter humour. I remember I once saw him laugh at a joke—although I really don't know if it was a joke—told by a friend called Jack Speakman who died early, but before my father, of pneumoconiosis. It involved a man on holiday in Morecambe. He is on the promenade. As he gazes out to sea he sees a stranger splashing about in the waves. 'Help', yells the man. 'I can't swim. I can't swim'. The holidaymaker from Wigan listens carefully as the drowning man continues to yell. 'For God's sake, some-one. Help me, won't you? I can't bloody swim. I can't bloody swim'. As the drowning man goes under for the last time the Wiganer shrugs his shoulders and turns to his mate. 'I cawnt ride a bike', he says. 'But I'm not shawting about it'.

If Wiganers have a sly preference for reticence and mockery over the razzamatazz and exotic whingeing of a coral-beach culture like that of Queensland, I'm not entirely sure that it tells us very much about who we are as a Rugby League people. Nor does it mean that we ought to agree with Geoffrey Moorhouse that the victim is a figure of secondary impor-tance in the history of the game. There is something prescriptive in the way Moorhouse complains about those who are guilty of 'collective resentment', as if they belong outside the game and have no right of expression within it. As he puts it: 'It is the whingeing, embittered character holding on to grudges who concerns me most of all . . . for he is an unlovely manifestation in our game and we ought to have outgrown him by now'.[4]

The remark is admirable and, if different circumstances obtained, one might wish that it were true. But it isn't true and there is nothing to say that it should be, or can be,

nor is there any evidence that most of us have managed to escape our 'grudges', or would do even if we wanted to (or would know what to do even if we had). Instead, we disguise the range of our 'grudges', many of which are necessary to us and define our ideals and historic purposes. We flatter ourselves with a mythology that teaches us to accept the virtue of passivity and amelioration, to sublimate whatever anxiety bedevils us within a condition of dignified silence. Only by accepting, so we say, the tradition that saw our parents through the worst excesses of the industrial revolution can we preserve the instinctive morality that binds together the people of Britain and hold the line against social overturning at a time when many of our faiths and indigenous traditions are at risk of being lost. What Rugby League offers, we say, is an alternative version of the rural idyll. In this, communities grow through sturdy individualism and life is regulated by an inherent sense of tolerance and reasonable-ness. Here, there is always the sound of cows lowing and bells at dusk and birds in the hedgerows and the friendly banter of rustic locals after a day at hay or cricket. But the idyll, as Martin Kettle has shown us, is deeply flawed and is often used as a means of keeping people in their place.[5] Its evasiveness lies in its refusal to acknowledge the actuality of politics beyond neighbourhood ideals, to admit the existence of real incompatibilities of interest and real social problems not susceptible to individual solution.

The search for a vanished innocence is a favourite theme of all communities in times of tension or prolonged economic recession. The search is conservative for it seeks to disentangle the psychic complexities of the moment by purging nature and society of their mysteries and by affirming the value of self reliance and eternal persistence. By identifying the 'atmosphere' at a typical Rugby League ground as one of 'cordiality, good humour and sportsmanship', Geoffrey Moorhouse identifies who we are, not through a paranoid or charismatic style (which, it seems to me, is perfectly acceptable) but by choosing to highlight the downbeat decorum that is lacking in the likes of Wally Lewis and the bananabenders of Queensland.[6] The definition omits as much as it implies. One could equally argue that moderation and tolerance are euphemisms for resignation and that an affable manner is simply a characteristic of those who refuse to take life seriously, especially in a world where the opportunities for radical achievement and self expression appear limited.

An easy going manner may also suggest a lack of personal assertiveness, the rigidity of a class expressing itself in an absence of ambition on a national stage. What other reason is there, one might ask, for our chronic inability to beat the Australians beyond the fact that there aren't enough of us who play Rugby League? And isn't the reason simply this, that for the best part of the twentieth century we have lacked the self confidence to promote our game and attract sufficient numbers of youngsters into it? Instead, we have channelled our aspirations and confined our ambitions to a narrow corridor of the M62. We have become, some might say, the cowed practitioners of the art of rebellion, one-time dissidents who became deferential—bogged down by class reticence, bumbling incompetence and parochial self-interest. What stops us from spelling our deficiencies out? Mr. Moorehouse, for one, is unwilling to tell us. 'Why *should* it be thought desirable to expand?'[7] he asks.

The links between northernism and a culture of resistance are part and parcel of Rugby League folklore. What has occupied our attention less are the reverberations of 1895 and the impact of breakaway on our sense of class. One thing which might profitably be looked at, for example, is the way those with whom we severed our connections have chosen to define us in terms which imply the corruption of class. Resentment is the key. The clubs that seceded from the Rugby Football Union in 1895 were represented not merely by players who were northern and industrial and working class; but players who were talented, competitive and highly successful. Northern Rugby Union clubs were among the best in Britain during the early 1890s. The act of separation caused considerable anger in the south for the loss of the north proved extremely damaging to the reputation of the English Rugby Union and its ability to demonstrate imperial authority on the field of play. This anger expressed itself in many ways. No longer was the north of England, after 1895, seen as a place of outstanding natural talent. It was portrayed as a place with a natural inclination to disloyalty, a region where the spirit of class had become corroded by maverick attitudes and a too-close involvement with the needs of industry. The ideal of service, so it was argued, had disappeared from the north. The working-class labourers had given in to greed. What they now lacked was adequate moral supervision.

The emergence of Rugby League did not result in the break up of class definition in British sport nor did it undermine the meaning of the term 'working class' as a referent that carried with it a highly emotive trace or tail. On the contrary, the tail tended to lengthen and the word northernism became a term of abuse in Rugby Union circles, a synonym for those whose lives were regulated by the incessant rhythm of the industrial machine. While other working-class regions of Britain found that the Rugby Football Union tended to identify them in more favourable terms, Rugby League clubs heard themselves referred to as a social menace, institutions where the moral reprobates of the world could gather together and become contaminated with the virus of commercialism.

The response of the Rugby Football League, over the years, has been complex and contradictory. In the decade after 1895 the game quickly established itself as dynamic and popular. It was able to attract large numbers of spectators and players from the ranks of Rugby Union and to seek liaisons with other rugby-playing nations like New Zealand and Australia. On the one hand the game sought to develop its traditions of dissent, rebellion and individuality and to define itself through changing patterns of experimentation on the field of play. In so doing, it thumbed its nose at the old-time bosses of the Rugby Football Union and actively sought to challenge the dominance of that code. Within a few years Rugby League had its sights set on new horizons and was willing to underwrite international tours.

The new organisation also became conscious of its status and of the need to display an authority of its own. Here it faced enormous problems since the game had chosen to distance itself from the stodgy traditionalism of the Rugby Union and the Victorian ethos of the public schools. In picking a fight with the southern middle class, the Northern Union was up against a strata of society that regarded itself as a defender of the nation's traditions, and one that was well able, because of its undoubted influence in the press, to adjudicate on matters of taste and morality at moments of crisis. The backlash against the game was considerable. The loss of domestic territory, as well as the loss of frontier or colonial territory in New Zealand and Australia, provoked a withering assault on 'the creeping imperialism' of Rugby League from those who defended the interests of Union. [8]

The legacy of 1895 posed other problems. While Rugby League continued to push back the frontiers there were those in positions of authority who caved in under the pressure to conform exerted by the Rugby Union. As the story of Dai Davies shows us, northern club officials occasionally backtracked on the democratic principles of 1895 preferring, instead, the rigid rhetoric of the authoritarian. Dai always said he could smell a rat whenever a committee man actively looked for respect from a player or presented himself as a true-blue believer in regimental authority. Dai's narrative introduces us to a variety of officials in Rugby League, many of them generous, decent and hardworking. But one cannot ignore the presence of those whom Dai came into conflict with, the insular and elitist snob who believed that the duty of the club was never to look outside itself or threaten the hegemony of Rugby Union. For such people to strain at the leash of obedience was a sin. To make waves would only cause offence to one's betters and bring the wrath of God upon the club. Wherever we look in Rugby League we see these officials. Whatever the period, we witness the disastrous evidence of their legacy: the spectacular timidity of the Bill Fallowfield era, the deferential jokiness of our media scribes, the bowing and scraping that often goes on in the company of the Rugby Union.

There has been, over a long period of time, a chronic failure of leadership in Rugby League, a failure of will and political conviction as well as an inability to develop the game in non-traditional areas of the country. The reason lies, I think, in the evolution of the boardroom figure over the last hundred years, a Darwinian specimen who has bottled himself in a peculiarly northern form of aspic. The Rugby League director is a genuine enigma; he is of the people yet above the people, a local lad made good who lacks the desire to leave his community yet wishes to do his best within it. He has a genuine love of the game and is willing to invest a fortune in his home town club in order to make it a focal point of civic pride. At the back of his mind he wishes to prove a point or two to the Rugby Union with whom he has a curious love-hate relationship, detesting its official pieties but admiring its players to such an extent that he is almost willing to bankrupt the club in order to get hold of them.[9] He is constantly looking for new ways to make his game more entertaining and he has little time for the intellectual —and what he considers sentimental—clap trap with which the 'kick and clap' code, as he refers to Rugby Union, coddles itself. He firmly believes in the symbolism of the chevron that Rugby League players wear on their jerseys. In medieval literature the chevron on a character's shield tended to imply a negative judgement, with oblique lines suggesting a deviation from the norm and sharp points the symbols of danger. For our director, Rugby League teams proclaim their transgression and the greater physical dangers that face those who play the professional code.

In reality, the political defiance of the official and the level of danger to which he is exposed is minimal. The Rugby League official is a playacting insurgent who rarely ventures out beyond the confines of the town to confront the adversary on his own turf. Nor is he asked to explain his philosophy to anyone other than those whose company he feels relaxed in. He buys from Rugby Union but does not debate the principle of purchase. Lacking the capacity for long-term constructive analysis of the game his instincts lead him, on occasion, to satisfy the short-term needs of his club by hammering at the door of every available Rugby Union player. (Just look at what happened in the 1980s.) Because he is unsure of his status in the wider world he is unwilling to venture into it. By seeking a position on a board of directors he looks for recognition in his own community but knows he won't get it in negotiations with the Rugby Union. Lacking the wit or the inclination to expand the game in unfamiliar regions he feels overwhelmed by—and a little clumsy in—a world that respects neither his name nor his chequebook. He develops a siege mentality yet remains ever keen to demonstrate his authority in the company of players and fellow officials. The ambition of the patriarch rotates inward; rarely, if ever, does he focus his attention on the political challenge thrown down by Rugby Union. Nor is he able in the quality or tabloid press to articulate a constructive and challenging definition of his game in order to refute Rugby Union propaganda. As is illustrated by the recent dispute between the British Amateur Rugby League Association and the Rugby Football League, the energy of the official tends to implode; it becomes an exercise in self importance. Nick Garnett illustrates the problem in an article he wrote for the *Financial Times* in 1985. Rugby League, he argues, 'has elevated parochialism into an art form'. It 'is a sport run largely by men whose insularity and lack of vision undermines expansion and ensures that its foothold in the south remains slippery'. Harry Edgar of *Open Rugby* agrees. 'No one [from Rugby League] has ever sat down and said this is where we want to go', says Edgar. 'No sport is achieving less of its potential. It's a great product in the wrong package'.[10] One hopes the arrival of Maurice Lindsay at Chapeltown Road will bring to an end, once and for all, this tradition of lacklustre administration and deference.

Rugby Union players have a particularly hard time in coming to terms with the contradictions of Rugby League. They are among the most highly paid and most easily victimised, always vulnerable either to bad advice, no advice or disinformation. The courage they require to do well is exceptional for they are obliged to encounter moments of extreme loneliness as well as the envy, suspicion and hostility of those who lack their privileges and publicity. Rugby Union players may be loved and adored, as Jim Sullivan was at Wigan, but the standards expected of them are far higher, I think, than of any other player, for their signing represents a considerable investment in time, money and public credibility on behalf of the club. Theirs is, as Nick Garnett puts it, 'a polar expedition without thermals'.[11]

The problem starts the moment they sign professional forms. The Rugby Union press goes for the jugular and, as if the player has suddenly become a more immediate threat to public order than a child molester or the I.R.A., applies the generic label of 'defector'. The sin of defection seems to exact its own retribution. The Rugby Union press point us to the experience of John Gallagher whose fate, they argue, was sealed by the jealousy his signing aroused among his fellow Rugby League players. That John Gallagher at Leeds may not have been up to it is discounted by Union journalists unable to contemplate that standards in League may sometimes be higher than those in Union.

A simpler explanation—and one that is rarely offered by Union journalists—is that those who fail to make the grade in Rugby League actually experience too little attention, not too much. The cold shoulder of isolation in Rugby League is a fairly common experience, as David Young found out when he moved from Cardiff to Leeds. At Leeds, Young was left to his own devices to learn as he went along the requirements of a position with which he was familiar but wholly unprepared for. He received little in the way of coaching and orientation, a belittling experience for any player to have to go through and one that did little for the credibility of the game. The same applies to the treatment given to the South African fisherman, Green Vigo, who came to Wigan in the 1970s. Vigo is a tragic example of a player who could barely speak a word of English on his arrival in Britain, yet he received minimal help and counselling from the club. In spite of a severe problem of cultural adjustment Vigo was allowed to gain a reputation as a man who was awkward, rebellious and undisciplined. And when, at last, he proved too hot to handle he was put on the list at Wigan and left to fend for himself. Green Vigo's experience was not exceptional, nor can it be said to lie outside the Rugby League mainstream. The man was a victim of culpable negligence. He is not, as is often thought, an exotic exhibitionist who lived on the periphery of a game he couldn't cope with.

The same is true, but to a lesser extent, of Dai Davies. When Dai left Neath in 1925 he joined a convoy in which hundreds of players from the valleys of South Wales headed north in one of the greatest migrations of sporting talent in British social history. At the time Dai was twenty-three years of age, although typically he told the newspapers he was only twenty-one. In Wales, Dai was street-wise but when he signed for Broughton he received an education—some of it brutal —in how to survive by living off your wits. When Dai signed for Broughton Rangers the club was on its uppers. It had precious little talent of its own yet it knew how to recognise a sucker when it saw one. For almost two years it pushed Dai to the limits of his endurance but offered him little in the way of coaching or counselling. Dai learned quickly. Unable to speak decent English when he arrived he had to learn to express himself, both on the field and off it. The reputation he established as Broughton's most dangerous player made him a marked man. After suffering a severe facial injury and repeated cuts in wages Dai confronted the club directors and demanded to be put on the transfer list. After some hesitancy the request was granted and he was transferred to Warrington where he was offered a much better contract, decent wages and a place on the first team.

Warrington was a club which prided itself on its family atmosphere and Dai thrived on the attention he received. In his first Rugby League Cup Final (at Wigan) he scored a try and his rapidly emerging talent soon attracted the attention of the international selectors. By the early 1930s he had established himself, without question, as one of the finest scrum halves in Britain. Yet things didn't go all his way and the strain of living away from Wales proved considerable. After moving to the north of England Dai's father broke the home up in Garnant and his mother died. In 1932, after two marvellous tour trials, his world came apart when he was overlooked for the Australian tour party, a decision that smacked, to Dai, of political duplicity at the highest level. In spite of these setbacks Dai stayed hungry for success. In 1933 he went to Wembley to play in the Rugby League Cup Final and scored two tries for Warrington. (According to Ernie Day, the Warrington historian, Dai would have won the man of the match by a mile if such a trophy had then been awarded.) Toward the back end of his career

he again went to Wembley with Huddersfield and Keighley but on each occasion he was denied a winner's medal.

To play Rugby League Dai Davies became an emigrant, a Welshman who transferred his allegiance from one code of rugby to another. In doing so he encountered many, if not all, of those social and sporting problems that Rugby Union players must face when they enter Rugby League. This is especially true of those who 'go north', as Dai did, from the cloistered world of the south Wales valleys where the village is the organic centre of society and English a second language. For such players the change to Rugby League can be traumatic. For one thing, they have no previous experience of any of the tensions that set Rugby League players apart and that give them such a separate and obsessive identity in the minds of those who disapprove of the game. Even the working-class Welshman of radical, political and class conviction can have no substantive knowledge of the enmity to which he will occasionally be subjected by the sneering fan or the journalist/ apologist or the embittered committee man from Rugby Union. What he enters is a world apart, a game whose perception of itself lacks the kind of neutral composure which is second nature in Rugby Union, one whose historic identity cuts the participant off from the past and seems to indicate that the act of emigration is indeed irreversible. To play Rugby League is to acquire the cultural baggage of the man on the margins; it is to experience a kind of psychic disorientation for which there is little adequate preparation except to listen to the snippets of gossip and the rumour of those who have gone before you. The Rugby Union player confronts the legacy of a turbulent history, whether he is aware of it or not. This experience will soon let him know how durable the political and class conflicts between the two codes have become, and how the varying strains of cultural hostility and suspicion, that originated in l895, have persisted throughout much of the twentieth century.

For its critics and detractors Rugby League is little more than a set of allegations, many of which are expressed through nuance and smear. Critics have acquired a knee-jerk habit of referring to the game, directly or indirectly, through the idiom of the money-grabbing mercenary. Dudley Wood, for example, in a letter to *The Times,* 13 May l993, talks about the virtue of the amateur ideal and the 'abuses' that take place. These he identifies as 'envy, greed and ambition'. Wood is referring to the presence of a monied element in his own game and, by implication, those very things which corrode the aspiration of the human spirit. Wood believes in the morality of exercise and truth through joy. Rugby Union, he says, is a 'healthy, highly energetic and enjoyable form of recreation in a disciplined framework for several hundred thousand young people'. [12]

This particular link between physical hygiene and moral health is a well-roasted chestnut pulled out of the fire by the Rugby Union whenever there is a whiff of scandal in the air. The style is universal. At a time when the leading players in New Zealand are, according to Robert Armstrong of *The Guardian,* reputed to be earning £40,000 a year as members of the All Blacks Club, the New Zealand R.F.U. skilfully deflect any criticism of this trend by employing Michael Jones, the All Black flanker, to travel round the country as the evangelist of amateurism. Jones, claims Armstrong, is a decent Christian whom God has instructed to go forth and preach the gospel. Jones, he says, is a figurehead in Rugby Union. He is 'unique' and 'colossal'; so close is he to God that the other All Blacks 'lower their voices when they join his company'. When spoken to, Jones reveals all. 'My Christian faith adds another dimension to being an All Black', he says, 'so it's important for me to do my best'. Rugby Union makes this possible: the translation of faith, the expression of charisma. 'Faith and rugby are both disciplines and through rugby I have learnt a lot about myself and my life'. Jones is a 'colossus', 'the greatest open-side flanker the game has produced', and he has devoted himself not merely to God but to the gospel according to Rugby Union. Sometimes, of course, it's not always easy to figure out which particular hymn Jones is singing. The word of rugby in Jones's liturgy seems to be synonymous with the word of God. But this, of course, isn't any old rugby and this, of course, isn't any old God! It's our God he's worshipping, says Armstrong, a Christian God, and it's our game he's playing, Rugby Union. It goes without saying that the tolerance and generosity of Jones the Christian does not allow him to embrace Rugby League. [13]

Articles like this cropped up at random during the course of this essay. There is nothing unusual or distinctive about them; each is fairly run of the mill and, by Rugby Union standards, not especially confrontational. Each is typical of the innuendo journalism that the Rugby Union hack specialises in, belittling Rugby League through pious disdain. In reading these articles the Rugby League fan feels unwelcome, as if he has suddenly strayed off-limits, taken the wrong tour guide, entered the cathedral instead of the mosque. The self confidence of the writing reeks of exclusivity. It is carved from fine-grained mahogany. It speaks to the reader about the righteousness of a church whose style of worship is deeply authoritarian.

According to the schoolteacher in Toni Morrison's *Beloved* 'definitions belong to the definers—not the defined'.[14] For Rugby League, the attempt to escape the imprisoning reference of elite 'definitions' has proved a virtually impossible task over the last hundred years. Without the network of cultural and media connections, especially in the quality press, Rugby League has lacked adequate resources to define itself. The absence of voice and representation has put the game at an enormous disadvantage in a sporting environment dominated by those who publicise the interests of Rugby Union. The sense of occasional inferiority which this breeds gives us the appearance and sometimes the outlook of a third-world culture. It also gives us, a kind of existential strength, an inner conviction which has allowed us to generate an embattled camaraderie.

The problem is that the game has not always realised its strength or known what to do with its vast potential. The image of the victim remains a debilitating burden for the game's administrators. So durable is the myth of our marginal status and so pervasive are the doubts about our credibility as a legitimate alternative to Rugby Union that we tend on occasion not to question them. When the BBC uses the word 'rugby' in order to describe Rugby Union, it seems to cause us too little pain, for we are not sufficiently sensitive to the offence. Whenever this happens I rarely hear anyone say that the BBC is rewriting history.

If Rugby League is to survive beyond the next twenty years—and escape the inevitable co-option of its skill by a predatory Rugby Union—it must learn to reclaim the past, much of which has been stolen, and to refute the definitions and misleading identities that are often ascribed to it. One way of doing this is to write history, as Barbara Christian puts it, 'from the inside out'.[15] That is, to do what African-American, Chicano and Native American writers have done for their own communities in the United States over the past twenty years. Here, the achievement has involved nothing less than the reinscription of an entire ethnic history in order to expose the structure of lies and disinformation on which a hegemonic culture has often relied in order to demean it. The task has been accomplished in each of these communities by the writer acting as a folk historian, as someone who reinvents the past through the language of the tribe and the gossip of the street. By letting the fiction filter through to the reader through the imagination of an ancestor figure the historical record is authenticated in traditional terms. The indigenous voice confirms the power of oral testimony at worm's-eye level; it conveys the need for ethnographic specificity in the reinvention of the past.

As a minority sport Rugby League has long struggled to make itself heard. According to Geoffrey Moorhouse the lack of a clear and distinctive voice has been exacerbated by the pitiful blandness of the various biographies of famous people who have played Rugby League: Gus Risman, Vince Karalius, David Watkins, etc. The writers of these books, says Moorhouse, come across as 'much the same as their counterparts in other sports; that is, artlessly repeating mostly well-known details of the subject's personal persona, but conveying almost nothing about him as a human being'.[16] The long-term effect of the typical biography is culturally disastrous, for it neutralises our sense of who we are in history. By hiding the links between identity and place or identity and language the ghost biography undermines authenticity and our need to express ourselves as individuals. It also encourages others to demean us, to look at us in much the same way that

Morrison's schoolteacher assesses his slaves —as a people 'whose neigh and whiny could not be translated into a language responsible humans spoke'.[17]

The idea of who speaks for whom, in what language and on what issues, derives from a need to subvert the identities that are given to us in the past. If we are what we are taught, then much of what we have been taught about Rugby League—and are still being taught on a daily basis—is incorrect. To counter this we must begin to explore, in the words of Toni Morrison, our 'interior life'. Testimony and witness must become the central concerns of our art. Only those whose work has the mark of authenticity on it, the approved credentials of race and class, and whose experience is the sign of immersion that certificates the memory and renders it true and distinctive, can replace what the Nigerian writer Chinua Achebe describes as the 'short, garbled, despised history of third world people'.[18] It is this belief in an ethnographically correct representation of culture that sustains the Chicana novelist Sandra Cisneros when she says of her upbringing in Chicago: 'You knew some things growing up in your communities that heads of state are never going to see. And once you've seen it, you can't unknow it… What you know at a very early age gives you empathy and compassion'. Behind this argument lies the belief that you cannot articulate what you do not understand, nor can you convey an experience that you have not actively shared with others, especially if you are the product of a community which, itself, has been 'denied achievement'.

Contemporary writers of colour, says Toni Morrison, 'are the subjects of [their] own narrative, witnesses to and participants in [their own] experience'. For these writers personal testimony and the act of bearing witness is no longer thought of as a disability.

'When I was eleven years old in Chicago', says Sandra Cisneros, 'teachers thought if you were poor and Mexican you didn't have anything to say. Now I think that what I was put on the planet for was to tell these stories because if I don't write them, they're not going to get the stories right'.[19] In order to correct the errors of a badly transcribed history, Maxine Hong Kingston describes her intention in *The Woman Warrior* as that of a 'daring talker of the tribe'. The need to record history through personal testimony is best appreciated, she says, by those who belong to minority communities. 'I liked the Negro students [Black ghosts] best', she announces, 'because they talked the loudest and talked to me because I was a daring talker too'.[20]

Like Maxine Hong Kingston, Dai Davies was a loud and 'daring talker of the tribe'. His voice is something we no longer hear nor is his silence a matter of regret. We prefer the world of words used loosely, the bland anonymity of the ghost biography, the lucid smoothness of the Union scribe for whom men like Dai are known as 'defectors'. To allow this language to go unchallenged is to reinvent the story of who Dai was, what Dai did and the reason he did it; it is, in effect, to brand him a traitor.

Below is a brief extract from an article written by David Irvine which appeared in *The Guardian* on 17 February 1993. It concerns the decision by Nigel Heslop of Orrell Rugby Union club to accept the offer made to him by Oldham's Peter Tunks of a match by match 'incentive' contract in Rugby League.

> Orrell, hemmed in all sides by some of the top professional clubs, have been bled for years— although, with most of their losses being at colts level, no one outside the club has taken much notice. More recently, however, defections have had a direct bearing on the first team.

They [the Rugby League scouts] are never far away, and we know lots of our lads are being constantly talked to. [21]

The problem of health, moral and physical, is once again in evidence; note the metaphors of bleeding (loss of fluid) and defecting (loss of spirit or belief). All forms of illness, it seems, which derive from the playing of Rugby League, are induced by the presence of parasitical or viral agents which cause a loss of bodily fuction and a breakdown in defence mechanisms. There is also the loss of emotional function to consider, for if players like Heslop are seduced by 'money' then the 'lads' in the 'colts' team are flattered by the attention they receive from the scout. Although they may not want to, these 'lads' are 'under pressure to switch codes'. The scout is relentless. He encourages the youth of Orrell to betray their allegiance to the cause and to abandon their belief in a game which has selflessly taught them all it knows. The scout is a wraith-like figure, a shadow-presence who exerts a menacing and unhealthy influence on the young and innocent. Wherever he goes he spreads a sinister aura of disloyalty.

The idea of Rugby League as virus or contagion and Rugby Union as shelter or nest is also conveyed by the Sports Editor of the *Western Mail*, John Kennedy, in a 1990 article he wrote on the scouting activities of Rugby League clubs in the Welsh valleys. Kennedy warns us of a 'new and frightening trend', a series of 'raids' which, he claims, are now being made by 'the Rugby League predators'. These aliens 'have chosen to target the cream of our schoolboy talent', the traditional academies of sporting excellence like Christ College and Llandovery. Kennedy's article consists of a series of lurid tales which tell the reader what it's like to live as a scout in the Rugby League underworld; how the scout is condemned to wander the street in a dirty raincoat on the lookout for talent—the 'lads' of Wales. [22]

The emotive language and the accusations contained in both articles are fairly commonplace. That both journalists use similar metaphors to illustrate the same offence says something about the uniformity of the Rugby Union mind. What is also curious is the way the nature of the offence changes as the 'lads' grow older and turn into men. Once an adult turns to Rugby League he commits the unpardonable sin of selling his body to the highest bidder. Here the act of transfer is mercenary. As Wilf Wooller put it in *The Sunday Telegraph* in 1985: 'The words "going north" carry emotive overtones in Wales. To switch to the professional code of Rugby League—as Cardiff's Terry Holmes did last week—is to defect: not only from amateur Rugby Union itself, but from your roots'. [23]

By choosing the verb 'to defect' the commentator anticipates the subsequent discrimination which the act of switching one's allegiance provokes. By 'going north' the player, as Nick Garnett puts it, 'risks becoming an historical non-person in the game [Rugby Union] that bred him. For the heinous crime of turning to another, if related, sport and receiving money doing so, the union hierarchy still takes a sour and bloody-minded view'. [24] The verb 'to defect' replaces the person with a moral condition. It makes him the victim of an experiment in disinvention.

In the act of rejecting the freemasonry of Rugby Union the convert to Rugby League casts himself in the role of the ante bellum slave who escapes the 'protection' of the southern family and takes the underground railroad. In so doing he becomes a kind of treacherous nigger, swapping his protection for a freedom of action he neither knows nor understands; he becomes a sporting pariah who willingly abandons the rights and privileges normally afforded to those who swear an allegiance to 'the family'. 'The sin of crossing cultures' is inexcusable. The player who does so can no longer expect to be rewarded through more acceptable forms of payment—car-park takings or the proverbial boot money.

Union journalists are partisan to the point of paranoia whenever they spot a 'defector' heading North. Those who get their retaliation in first resort to a kind of apocalyptic prophecy with lurid tales of moral decline. In Swansea, where I live, the local Petulengro of the tealeaves goes by the name of Martin Pitchwell, 'Wales' Most Outspoken Sports Writer'. In the weeks following the decision of Jonathan Davies to sign for Widnes, Pitchwell's readers were offered a sample of teacup tragedies and a heady brew of tales from the slop bucket. Pitchwell knew from his reading of the leaves what Widnes had in store for the luckless Davies. Staring into the murky recesses of an eleven o'clock cup of Tesco's Darjeeling Pitchwell announced that the 'attraction of Rugby League' was difficult to fathom. 'It seems so unsubtle—people running straight into other people for most of the time, then getting up, glaring, and back-heeling the ball to somebody else'. What the Indian weed revealed to Pitchwell is that 'every so often you are penalised if you do that, so you have to kick the ball instead, so it's predictable even then'. Under the intense glare of such a profoundly analytical mind the dark mysteries of Rugby League were gradually exposed like some noxious, swampy, primeval substance. 'The finer points' of Rugby League, 'if there [are] any', pass him 'by' because the game is predicated on the need for 'sheer ruthlessness'. It is played with a neanderthal primitivism that artists and visionaries find it difficult to adjust to. Jonathan will be a target. 'He will be hounded, pounded, goaded, insulted, bullied, scorned and, if the northern hard men have their way, humiliated in the next few weeks. He needs all the luck going'.[25]

In Rugby Union futurology what awaits 'the defector' is a level of pain so severe that his moral, physical and emotional self will simply disintegrate. The player will go through an experience known only to the most traumatised of coke sufferers, speed freaks and skid-row junkies. What Davies has done contradicts not only his own nature but every known rule of sporting logic.

Not that we would consider applying the same argument to the experience of other sportsmen. When Paul Gascoigne decides he wants to up sticks for Italy we do not say that he is choosing to enter the crime capital of Europe or is risking his sanity in the company of the Mafia. When John Surtees leaves motorcycling for car racing he is not accused of wanting to risk life and limb in some needless spectacle on the streets of Monte Carlo. When an amateur boxer quits the ranks of the A.B.A. and signs up as a professional we do not tell him that he is bound to suffer the obligatory fate of the punch drunk and brain damaged. Nor when Jeremy Guscott decides to become a male model do we say that he is about to rub shoulders with suspected Aids sufferers. When a bird decides to leave its nest or a wave chooses to separate itself from the anonymity of the ocean and crash upon the shore, or when a man wants a sex change or a film star an implant, we do not say that each has broken some inalienable law of God and abandoned their pre-ordained role in life. We accept the decision for what it is. Sometimes we may even marvel at it.

Freedom of expression is a wonderful

thing, except in rugby. Here it is considered a gross violation of natural law and the act of transfer is usually described as a horror-pornography. One thinks of the response of Dr. Dannie Craven when Ray Mordt and Rob Louw left South Africa and signed for Wigan in 1985. According to Paul Martin writing from Pretoria, Craven 'issued a seemingly non-stop barrage of gloom and doom messages to potential "traitors". He said they "would lose their freedom of action and become ensnared into slavery—able to be bought and sold like cattle"'. According to Martin, Craven 'also claimed' the players 'would have no career structure to fall back on once discarded or injured and that they would become (or rather, he would insist that they become) ostracised by the game that made them great. "They will experience the strictest form of apartheid—between Rugby Union and Rugby League—which have been sworn enemies for a century"'. Finally, Craven warned Louw and Mordt about injuries in Rugby League, 'adding that some players... "would be killed in the first few minutes"'. Dannie Craven was, as we all know, one of nature's gentlemen, a man who had no time for the language of apartheid, sporting or racial, a real home-on-the-range gent who spent his life in the forefront of the struggle for racial equality in South Africa and who committed himself to upholding the principles of natural justice, freedom of expression and civil rights for all. As Jack McNamara puts it: 'You'll remember that this grand sport once described Rugby League players as "reptiles". A lovely bloke! I puked when I read the sycophantic obits'.[26]

With some exceptions, like Clem Thomas,[27] the vilification of Rugby League is a traditional strategy for the elder statesmen of Rugby Union. In 1977, Gordon Mackintosh, President of the Lancashire R.F.U., complimented Orrell on the club's success in recent years: 'As President of Lancashire', he announced at the club's annual dinner, 'I am proud of Orrell. It is good to know that rugby in this part of the world is in very safe keeping. We live in a world of curious standards, which are sometimes cheap and sleazy, but you at Orrell have become the guardians of rugby'.

Mr. Mackintosh's speech distinguishes between that which is Orrell—where 'rugby is played' and standards are in 'safe' hands—and that which is not Orrell, where 'rugby' is not played and the prevailing standards are, as he puts it, 'cheap and sleazy'. Orrell, as every rah-rah supporter knows, lies in the middle of an indigestible rugby sandwich, the nutritional value of which is ruined by the 'cheap and sleazy' crust of professionalism. Either side of Orrell one finds the denial of wholesome and healthy 'standards' and the absence of fruitful organic relationships, the kind of which Mr. Mackintosh finds in abundance at Orrell. Mr. Mackintosh directs us to an old idea in the moral folklore of Rugby Union: the idea that Rugby Union is a moral union against those 'cheap and sleazy' values which threaten to overwhelm 'those parts of the world' that play Rugby Union.[28] The people of Orrell are the 'guardians' of rugby and Edge Hall Road is a noble outpost where the sacred flame of Twickenham is cherished on a postage stamp of English soil. Either side of Orrell are the menacing industrial townships of Wigan and St. Helens, centres of heathenism, secularism and anti-ruralism.

The argument that Rugby Union is an ethically uplifting activity is regularly parroted by a variety of stooges. When Fergus Slattery says that Rugby Union is hygienic because it's amateur—'We play in a very healthy atmosphere and I believe that we owe this to the fact that our game is strictly amateur'[29]—he indulges in a typical Union conceit in which amateurism is defined one way and experienced another (not as the absence of financial reward but as the absence of visible, financial transaction). Those who subscribe to the principles of Rugby Union are not necessarily opposed to the idea of money nor are they opposed to the values of capitalism. Rugby Union people are not known for their impoverished status, their ascetic ideas, their primitive values or their anti-materialism. On the contrary, the Rugby Football Union has probably the largest collection of active and well-heeled capitalists of any sporting organisation in Britain. The problem, therefore, is not with money as a medium of exchange or with the idea of monetary reward for services rendered.[30] The problem, historically, is in allowing money to fall into the wrong hands: in allowing those who have found themselves to be deprived of money, or lacking in money, to earn it for themselves without the prior approval of those who, traditionally, are known to control the supply of it. Money becomes 'dirty', therefore, when the need to acquire it becomes more important than a willingness to obey the rules of those who have never been deprived of it. Money, in other words, acquires a loaded moral status when earned by the wrong people in the wrong place and in the wrong game—those who lack the certification of authority or the appropriate credentials of birthright, education and class. The idea that money can be a viral pollutant with subversive properties when used indiscriminately and in ways that do not conform to the socio-political tastes of an elite, is a fiction that is bought into by many elite people in the Union game, including the Irish like Fergus Slattery.

Broken-time payments were of vital importance to men working six days a week in mills, foundries and coal mines in the 1890s. To play rugby instead of working meant forfeiting a wage and although the north of England in the 1890s was producing the finest rugby players in the country—the backbone of the England Rugby Union team —few of these players could afford the luxury of taking time off to play on a Saturday. The rule-makers of English rugby, men from the middle and upper classes, did not require reimbursement for loss of wages and were perfectly able to 'take time off from their properties, their businesses and professions whenever they had a mind to play games, to go fishing, to hunt fox, to shoot birds'.[31] These men experienced a considerable degree of pique when a number of clubs in the north of England refused to accept the prevailing convention that those who played Rugby Union should grin and bear the loss of wages they incurred on a Saturday.

The decision by the rule-makers to sever all links with the Northern Union was the natural reaction of a class that regarded itself an unimpeachable authority on matters of taste and morality. This was a time, as Noel Annan puts it, when 'the restraints of religion and thrift and accepted class distinction [had] started to crumble and English society to rock under the flood of money'.[32] The action of the Northern Union was regarded as the thin end of the wedge by those members of the establishment who prided themselves on their gentlemanly capitalism, their sense of decorum and their reputation as purveyors of Victorian stability and middle-class virtue. Given the loss of Corinthian soccer to the working classes, officials of the Rugby Union were highly sensitive to the possibility of losing control of yet another bastion of amateur Englishness, especially to a bunch of provincial barbarians. It was entirely befitting that a man of the cloth like the Reverend

Frank Marshall should set his sights firmly against unwelcome strangers. The money men of Lancashire and Yorkshire, he argued, inflamed the ambitions of lads of rudimentary knowledge whose moral welfare the game of Rugby Union had always claimed responsibility for. Marshall propagated the received wisdom of yet another man of the cloth, the Reverend William Webb Ellis—he who had preached the gospel of amateurism earlier in the century to the public schools.

In the nineteenth century Rugby Union was at the centre of what Martin J. Wiener has called the 'rural myth' of Victorian imperialism. Public schools, many of which were set in the countryside in order to hold 'the urban industrial world at arm's length', were attended by the sons of clergymen and the landed gentry. This was a leisured class which actively discouraged the acquisition of technical and professional skills and was openly disparaging of the world of business. In the early years of the nineteenth century public schools were 'little more than finishing schools for sons of the landed gentry'. When Tom Brown, son of an idealised country squire in *Tom Brown's Schooldays* (1857), expresses a wish to 'be at work in the world' rather than go up to Oxford, he is corrected by a master who tells him that whatever happens he must not 'drop into mere money-making'. In a later Victorian novel about Harrow, Horace Vachell's *The Hill* (1905), a businessman's child arrives at school under a cloud of suspicion. Though rising by his ability to captain the cricket team he remains an outsider and ends by being expelled for dishonesty. 'One is sometimes reminded', another boy comments, 'that he is the son of a Liverpool merchant, born in or about the docks'.[33] If honesty is associated with rural culture, civilised values and Englishness, and if Britain in her hour of greatest need has

always been saved (or so we are told) by the representatives of the public schools then, by implication, those who choose not to subscribe to the moral authority of the gentry are treacherous and untrustworthy. In this mythology the north becomes a place of desperate competition characterised by a cynical win-at-all-cost attitude, in contrast with the south of England which is the pastoral domain of Britain and the repository of a benevolent and civilised disposition. For this reason, southern England had a very high proportion of the most prestigious public schools whose inherent sense of fair play, it was thought, made them better able to cope with life's trials and stresses. This equation between the spirit of fair play and public-school sport—cricket, especially—was established by Sir Henry Newbolt in his poem 'Vitai Lampada', a public-school favourite in the 1890s:

> There's a breathless hush in the Close tonight
> Ten to make and the match to win—
> A bumping pitch and a blinding light,
> An hour to play and the last man in.
> And it's not for the sake of a ribboned coat,
> Or the selfish hope of a season's fame,
> But his Captain's hand on his shoulder smote—
> 'Play up! play up! and play the game'.

In later life, the former cricket brave exhorts his colonial troops beset by natives:

> The sand of the desert is sodden red—
> Red with the wreck of a square that broke;
> The Gatling's jammed and the Colonel dead,
> And the regiment blind with dust and smoke;
> The River of death has brimmed his banks,
> And England's far, and Honor a name;
> But the voice of a schoolboy rallies the ranks;
> 'Play up! play up! and play the game'.

Donald Horne, in a fascinating study of British identity, draws our attention to the cultural legacy of two competing geographic myths. In the Northern Metaphor, says Horne,

> Britain is pragmatic, empirical, calculating, Puritan, bourgeois, enterprising, adventurous, scientific, serious, and believes in struggle. Its sinful excess is a ruthless avarice, rationalised in the belief that the prime impulse in all human beings is a rational, calculating, economic self-interest. In the Southern Metaphor Britain is romantic, illogical, muddled, divinely lucky, Anglican, aristocratic, traditional, frivolous, and believes in order and tradition. Its sinful excess is a ruthless pride, rationalised in the belief that men are born to serve.

In the contest that took place throughout the nineteenth century as to which Britain was best, 'it was the Southern Metaphor that won', says Wiener. By the turn of the century it was commonly believed among elite political and cultural circles that British success in the world was 'due not so much' to the labouring efforts of the industrial north as to the 'unique cultural inheritance' of the south; in other words, not to the plebian ideal of productivity but the gentlemanly virtue of duty and service.

The idea of 'provincialism in twentieth-century Britain', says Wiener, 'has not been simply a matter of remoteness from the capital city... it has been much more a question of remoteness from [an] approved style of life'. If the virtue of Englishness was the virtue of the country, then to live outside the metaphor of Englishness was to live away from that which was rural. 'Provincialism [was] to live in or near an industrial town to which the industrialised revolution gave its significant modern form'.[34] Thus, while Twickenham presents itself as a bastion of southern power and imperial construction, 'the last fortress of the Forsytes', the grounds of Rugby League are designed to emphasise the provincial virtues of modesty and suburbanism. Rugby League grounds, says Geoffrey Moorhouse, express an organic relationship between the spectator and his environment, whilst Twickenham was created as a 'prestige ground' in an 'empty' but salubrious 'corner' of Middlesex. Twickenham, says Moorhouse, has nothing to do with the historical 'attachment' of the fan to the community.[35]

The industrial image of Rugby League which proves so offensive to the sense and sensibility of Rugby Union has a profound mythological and psychic resonance. In 1992 England played Canada in a Rugby Union international at Wembley stadium, a place which holds a special affection for Rugby League fans. Except for once during the war the Rugby Union has never bothered with Wembley as a sporting venue, but on this occasion it did condescend to visit the stadium and, incidentally, produce a game of mind-numbing mediocrity. Enter John Hopkins, Rugby correspondent of the *The Financial Times, Times* and *The Observer*. Hopkins' report in *The Observer* consisted of an imaginary conversation with his son to whom he describes, not the game, but the stadium: 'All porcelain lavatories and hot air machines to dry your hands'. There is no 'singing' at Wembley, says Hopkins to the lad. Twickenham, however, has 'a special atmosphere', one that greets you the moment you arrive in the car park and 'enjoy' yourself on 'champagne, red wine and paté' from the car. 'None of this' is possible at Wembley, a stadium which 'looks as though it is set in the middle of an industrial area'. No wonder the northerners like it so much. Here is a gigantic Wheeltappers and Shunters Social Club, 'a journey across continents' from the leafy, garden suburb of Twickenham. 'It is hard to get enthusiastic' about Wembley, says

Hopkins, when all you can smell is the aroma of mass culture, 'the pervading smell of Fish & Chips, Sausage & Chips, Chicken & Chips, Hamburgers & Chips. Chips with everything in other words'. Wembley is a place where the products of mass culture are tastelessly packaged and avidly consumed. The ambience of the location is not conducive to an authentic folklore. It is a place of deracinated activity and pure functionalism. [36]

In the mythology of its supporters Rugby Union is the game of the garden, a reminder of merry England when battles were won on the playing fields of Eton. Even in areas like south Wales where the landscape is often heavily industrialised and the politics closer to those of the north of England, there still exists a yearning for the rural. This is often represented in the press as a romantic attempt to retrieve an ancestral memory, a desire to capture a spirit of lost youth on 'fields of praise', a vision of loveliness that once was Wales before industry came and the valleys changed from green to black. In playing Rugby Union, the Englishman's game, a curious act of collusion takes place beween two sentimental traditions. What we find is a common celebration of ruralism that is infinitely more interesting than the demonstrations of tribal conflict which Rugby Union matches between England and Wales are supposed to generate. When the Welsh visit London for the England/Wales game they press the flesh and understand the connections. They conspire to define their cultural and social identity through the playing of an English, public schoolboy's game. In so doing, they announce their refusal to go the way of the north of England. They play footsy with Twickenham Toryism and the gentleman capitalists of the south. And their pay-off is considerable. Although the landscape of Wales has many of the same ecological features as the North of England—the moors/the valleys, the mines/the mills—one rarely, if ever, hears it described by Union commentators in quite the same way as the north of England. If Wales is tragic it is also romantic. High on aspiration. Innate genius. The spirit of Glyndŵr. It is a place of valleys and chapels and hymns and arias; little old ladies who eat leek soup and tough, tough, men made of granite and anthracite whose belly breathes fire with the *hwyl* of the dragon. This is no scrap-heap land, here are no kitchen sinks and neanderthal primitives, no Coronation Streets, no 'cruel northern pastures'. Wales is a place of fulfillment. To leave Wales for the north of England, is, as Mervyn Davies puts it when Jonathan Davies went north to Widnes, 'like putting a Renoir in the loo'.

The Welsh, like the English, see Rugby Union as a centre of order in a complex and rapidly changing world, a storehouse of recorded values, a reminder of an old stability. Rugby League, on the other hand, testifies to the growing power of an urban, citified, mercantile society: the city not just as a place of rapid, communal activity but as metaphor for a new kind of experience and a new secularity. In this mythology Rugby League contains a powerful assertion of the deprivation of past centres of value; the loss of the social cohesion and rhythms of an agrarian world and the ideas and wisdoms of an old bourgeoisie and their poetic-religious faith.

Franz Fanon, in writing about the literature and art of neocolonisation in *The Wretched of the Earth* (1961), shows that the culture of the dominant forces in society tends to portray colonised peoples as 'others'—as slaves (inferiors) or monsters (threats)—or it tends to marginalise them on the borders of historical memory. Excluded, they either become invisible or they are presented as aliens. Similarly, Pierre Macherey in *A Theory of*

Literary Production (1966), calls our attention to the phenomenon of structured absence in art; to the significance of what is left out of an event, to what has been forgotten or perhaps suppressed as our memory of the past is revised in accordance with a prevailing ideological drift.

The Rugby Football Union regularly tends to portray Rugby League as a game designed to suit the aspirations of a brutalised proletariat. It also seeks to disappear those versions of history which cannot be demeaned through the use of propaganda. The art of vanishing history—or what Toni Morrison calls disremembering—is a familiar strategy in Rugby Union historiography. The moment the Rugby Union 'defector' goes north, says Nick Garnett, he commits in the eyes of the union hierarchy the sin 'of turning to another, if related, sport' and earning his living dishonestly. 'The spreading practice of payments in union leaves its hierarchy untouched, but the sin of crossing cultures is another thing'.[37]

John Ravitale recalls his life as a Rugby Union player in Fiji in the 1960s. He describes how, after his so-called 'links' with Rugby League were publicised in the press, the Rugby Union tried to discredit him and ruin his relationship with his own family. After thirty years Ravitale remains bitter. 'I'll never forget that', he says. 'Even my family didn't talk to me. The Union was very powerful'.[38] Jim Brough had a similar experience. When he was in his seventies he donated his English Rugby Union jersy to Silloth Rugby Union club where he began his career. The club was immediately ordered to remove it by the Rugby Football Union because, later in his career, Brough had signed for Leeds Rugby League Club.

The attempt to discredit the amateur status of eighteen and nineteen year old students was something I witnessed for almost fifteen years as a Rugby League coach and administrator in Wales. Before the free gangway between amateur Rugby League and Rugby Union came into being in the late 1980s, students who played Rugby Union on Saturday and Rugby League on Sunday were regularly informed that their chances of climbing the Rugby Union tree would be seriously jeopardised if they continued to play student Rugby League. I can think of at least twenty students—international players in both codes —who enjoyed the opportunity that Rugby League offered them to enhance their skills, yet who were regularly given the whisper-in-the-ear treatment by their Rugby Union coach (many of them physical education lecturers whose job it was to encourage the idea of freedom of sport within education). The students would be told to 'remember which side your bread is buttered on, son' or, 'I might not be able to stop you from playing Rugby League but I can certainly stop you from playing Rugby Union. I won't pick you'—a comment that was once made at South Glamorgan Institute. Such brave 'advice', intimidation masking as paternalism, was common currency in Wales during the 1980s.

Of course many of these coaches were simply taking their cue from the top, from the archpriests of discrimination in the Welsh Rugby Union. The need to witchhunt the young and put the frighteners on students stemmed from a paranoid suspicion that many of these 'lads' would be compelled against their wishes to switch to Rugby League in order to indulge in some satanic black mass. There was a regularly voiced horror story that went the rounds in the '80s that the students would be persuaded by myself, or Danny Sheehy in Aberavon, or Clive Griffiths in St. Helens, to throw in their lot with the devil himself and become 'professionals'. This never happened.

Whether it did or it didn't is beside the point. The treatment the students received and the way they persevered with Rugby League brings to mind a comment made by Geoffrey Moorhouse. When faced with Rugby Union discrimination, Moorhouse tells his reader to follow the advice of his grandmother and 'never mind them'. 'This', says Moorhouse, 'is not a bad way of disregarding those with whom you think you have irreconcilable differences. It has dignity'.[39] The students in Wales whom I knew had bags of dignity. They achieved an unprecedented level of success on the field and earned the title of European champions on several occasions. Yet, in spite of their achievement and the interest it aroused, the students refused to play to the gallery like Queensland's Wally Lewis. Because of this, their political problems were sometimes discounted or quietly buried and often by those who should have known better.

The attempt to discredit those who display an attachment to Rugby League has a timeless appeal for Rugby Union aficionados. In the early years of this century Ben Gronow played Rugby Union for Bridgend and Wales. In 1910 he signed for Huddersfield and played for the Rugby League Lions in Australia. When he retired he settled in Yorkshire and in the 1930s became the coach at Morley Rugby Union Club. In 1978 Morley held its centenary and in its brochure printed a picture of the 1936 Morley first team, including a head and shoulders shot of Gronow in the back row. Each person in the photograph is named with the exception of Gronow who is described as 'unknown'. When asked why the Morley club had done this, Henry Holliday, chairman of the club, said that it was necessary to 'forget' Gronow

in order 'to save embarrassment'. Holliday admitted he knew who Gronow was but didn't feel able to name him because 'the rulebook says that a player of his calibre should not be a coach for a Rugby Union club like ours'. (Note the words 'his calibre'.) The fact that Gronow had committed himself to Morley and given freely of his services as a coach in his later years meant nothing to the diehards. The men of Morley had not found it within themselves to honour and accept Gronow as one of their own. They denied the player his right to be remembered as well as his right to a name. In the photograph, Gronow lost not only his position in the club but also his position in society. Since he had no name he had no business being in the photograph. The absence of position signified intrusion; it reduced the coach to the status of a simpleton, a hanger-on in what appeared to be (in the centenary brochure) an exclusive event.[40]

The disappearance of the 'defector' is by no means an odd or freakish occurrence in Rugby Union circles. In the 1980s Nigel Starmer-Smith presented a feature on the sporting record of the Hesford family on 'Rugby Special'. Bob was described as playing Rugby Union for England and keeping goal for Blackpool F.C., while his sister was seen playing hockey for England. Brother Steve at the time was an outstanding fullback for Warrington but he never got a mention. 'I thought', says the journalist Jack McNamara, 'that if this was a mistake it was a bad one and if it was deliberate it was shameful'.[41] But, how does one shame a Rugby Union commentator? For the Union guru the emptying of minds and washing of hands is an act of faith. As time is rewound on the spool of memory we enter the world of Pol Pot's Year Zero. Ben Gronow and Steve Hesford have never existed. They inhabit the realm of the living dead, condemned to dwell in some underworld of perpetual exclusion. They are the 'No-Name' ghosts of rugby in Britain. Excluded from the proceedings of history, they are quietly erased from the sporting record.

Forgetfulness and wrongly attributed identity also feature strongly in the historiography of Rugby Union. Where, one asks, are the detailed accounts of the games that took place during the war years between players in both codes? Two particular instances come to mind, the first at Headingley, Leeds, on 23 January 1943, and the second at Odsal Stadium, Bradford, in 1944. Both matches were played under Rugby Union rules and both were organised by the armed forces at a time when League and Union players were granted a dispensation to play each other. The Rugby League team won on both occasions, at Headingley by 18-11 and at Odsal by 15-10. Although these matches were of great historic significance, they are given little serious attention in Rugby Union anthologies. In *The Playfair Rugby Football Annual 1948-1949*, the Headingley match is ignored, while the Odsal game is described as being 'not truly representative'. Yet, as the team sheets tell us, the Rugby Union sides contained a large number of seasoned internationals and were composed mainly of captains, majors, lieutenants from Oxford, Cambridge and the public schools. The Rugby League teams were made up of corporals, privates, gunners and troopers, lads who came from Castleford, Warrington, Dewsbury and St. Helens. It may be that the results proved a painful reminder of an earlier humiliation, the victories by Wales over the England Rugby Union team after the northern clubs seceded from the Union in 1895. A correspondent of the *Morning Leader* sums up the problem at the time:

For many years the Rugby Union has been a closed corporation, composed of men with the mistaken idea that only public schoolboys and University men could play the game. The middle-class and working-man footballer was barely tolerated. And yet it is the later class rather than the University player that furnishes the majority of the best footballers today. . . .[42]

Amnesia is a recurrent disability for the Rugby Union faithful when it comes to remembering events that took place, both at home and abroad, during the Second World War. Little attention has been given to what happened in Paris in 1941 when the French Rugby League was 'banned' and its assets liquidated by the Vichy government of Marshall Petain. The Vichy government, as Robert Fassolette has pointed out, were acting not only under the instructions of German command.[43] They were also responding to those politicians sympathetic to Rugby Union who wished to destroy the Rugby League game in France. 'Significantly', says Harry Edgar, 'Rugby Union was not banned—and during the war years Union clubs had their ranks boosted by many top league players, unable to take part in their own game'. Edgar continues:

The reason given for League being declared illegal by 'Vichy' included the allegation that Rugby League had many close links with England (significantly, at that time, the British home Rugby Unions had cut off their relations with France) and that Rugby League was a 'professional' sport and only amateur sports should be allowed to function during the war years.

But other 'professional' sports like football or cycling did not suffer the same fate as Rugby League. No other sport had its assets seized, no other sport had its offices (at that time in Bordeaux) burnt down and all its archives destroyed.[44]

The link between the Maquis, the rural resistance movement, and the villages where Rugby League was strong was well established. At an opportune moment the collaborators of Rugby Union were able to have the assets of the League Federation seized in order to deliver a fatal blow to the game's prestige. Once the war was over the Treizistes found it impossible to recover their former status, their assets lost and many of the clubs stripped bare by the Rugby Union. Much to the delight of defenders of the faith like Albert Ferrase, the Treizistes of the South eventually became the country cousins of French Rugby.

I do not wish here to go into the links that have long existed between the Rugby Union and totalitarian and right-wing governments. These have been well documented in various issues of *Open Rugby* since the mid 1970s, as has the overt and covert support given to apartheid regimes in white South Africa and the military juntas of Argentina.[45] The Welsh centenary tour of South Africa in 1989 caused such a storm of controversy that its repercussions are still being felt. The Pugh report based on a four-man committee of enquiry, leaked to the press at the end of 1991, painted not only a bleak picture of the way the tour had been organised, but raised serious allegations about an enormous cover up surrounding illicit payments made to ten of the players. The committee felt that 'on the balance of probabilities' and 'from the evidence heard … most and quite probably all the players were handsomely rewarded for going to South Africa'. In specific terms this meant that: 'At least one of the players received at least £30,000 and others as much or broadly comparable figures'. On that tour were current internationals such as Robert Jones and Mike Hall, the current team manager, Robert Norster, as well as other well-known South African aficionados such as Peter Winterbottom.[46]

It is here that a Rugby League person might be tempted to enquire about the depth of commitment in Rugby Union—a game which prides itself on its Corinthian amateurism, fair play and ecumenical philosophy—to multiracial activity. Where, for example, is the ethnic tradition in Rugby Union, the historiography and folklore of colour? Where do we go to in order to find it? Is it not an unpalatable fact that if we remove the few contemporary players of colour from the British Rugby Union game, what we are left with is a sea of irreducible whiteness? Where, one wonders, are the legions of black Rugby Union players? Why, for example, did the lads from Tiger Bay become famous at Rugby League instead of Rugby Union? Where are the Colin Dixons, the Johnny Freemans, the Billy Bostons, the Frank Wilsons, in the annals of the British Lions?

Dudley Wood has given us a timely answer. In 1993 he recently told a gathering of Sports Editors in London that British sport was overrun with black people and that their presence was a major turn-off for the public. Wood was targeting a number of sports, including Rugby League, which he said was 'bankrupt of ethics and ideas'. When accused by the sporting press of making racist remarks Wood argued that 'In Rugby Union we are very proud of the increasing flow of black players into the England teams'.[47] The one detail Wood forgot to acknowledge was that black people have never played Rugby Union in any significant numbers, nor, over the years, have they been encouraged to play. There is no tradition of colour in Rugby Union—no alternative lineage to that represented at international level in Rugby League by Ellery Hanley or John Ferguson, or Roy Francis. Instead, Rugby Union has been shaped by a racially conservative view of the world, one that is dominated by WASP values and cultural agoraphobia. Rugby League, on the other hand, a game often pilloried for its provincial values and its unwillingness to spread beyond a narrow, northern corridor, has wholeheartedly embraced the ideal of multiracialism throughout its history. The story of Rugby League is not, as one might imagine, that of the white, working class seeking to create a world unto itself. It is, to quote Maxine Hong Kingston, a story of 'outward tendencies', an infatuation with the possibilities of race and cosmopolitanism, coupled with a desire to investigate the borderless states that athletes of talent, whatever their background, are capable of achieving. Rugby League in Britain has thrived on a mixture of migrant flows and native traditions. Within the boundaries of the industrial town it has sought to blend together indigenous and immigrant cultures in new and experimental forms. Players of colour like Jason Robinson, Danny Wilson, Calvin Wilkes, Roy Powell, St. John Ellis, Des Drummond, Phil Ford, Anthony Sullivan, Ikram Butt, Hussein M'Barki, Alan Hunte, Eddie Rombo, Francis Jarvis—are just some of the more recent names who have made that experiment possible for the fans on the terrace.

When the Rugby Union talk of defection they wilfully obscure the spirit of openness in Rugby League. They falsify those traditions that have allowed many of the game's greatest figures—outsiders like Jim Sullivan and Brian Bevan—to be loved and accepted as if they were born and bred in the north. Here is the inexplicable paradox of Rugby League. The game finds itself unable to escape the imprisoning definitions of geography and class. It is riddled with parochial interests and anti-intellectualisms and dogged by feuds and tribal blood-letting. Yet, for all its faults, Rugby League remains admirably commited to a radical policy on matters of race, one that has recently taken it on a new adventure in the South African townships of Alexandria and Soweto.

Multiracial love affairs in Rugby League go back a long way, to the turn of the century, perhaps, and the maverick genius of James Peters ('Darkie Peters', as the R.F.U.'s official centenary history of 1970 refers to him). For others they begin with Cec Thompson or Roy Francis or even George Bennett. For me the story starts in 1953, the day I set eyes on W.J. Boston of Tiger Bay, Cardiff, as a six year old in Wigan. What Billy gave me was an education. And the fact that he was black made his presence in the town all the more important, especially at a time when immigrants were arriving in the north of England in serious numbers. Billy was the future. He blew into Wigan like a tropical storm and the place was never the same again. What Billy brought in was hurricane weather and the tidal wave that followed in his wake was as dark and frothy as medicine from Platts. Billy was turbulence. Whatever he brought got rid of the damp, the fog and smog of south-west Lancashire that puts coughing in the marrow when you're six years of age. You could feel the pressure as the ball went wide and the crowd rose up on a wave of its own. When Billy took off the crowd surged and the noise of the crowd was like wind that comes with a storm in the Gulf and then dies beyond the shoreline. What Billy brought in was a change of pressure. He was wind and fire from Tiger Bay and high-octane energy from the Caribbean. He was the outside world taking us apart, moving through us and then settling us again.

Nobody I knew talked to Billy. Nobody my age. There was this rumour that if you did want to talk to him you had to go to Poolstock Labour Club, even though that meant catching a bus when none of us had the money. Billy belonged to us in spite of Poolstock. I lived in Dicconson Street and Billy's brother, Herbert, came up from Cardiff and, for a while, he lodged by the park before they made the buildings into offices and got rid of the Aspeys and the Jolleys who lived in the slum parts and Peter Shields and George Young who could hit a thrush with a homemade knife at forty paces. There were some 'backs' between us and where Herbert lived and in the summer Herbert came out and we played cricket on a tarmac strip with gravel on the top. Herbert was friendly but it wouldn't have mattered even if he wasn't because Herbert was Billy's brother and Billy was someone everyone agreed on. Even the Catholics. Billy was ecumenical. Like Eddie Cochran, Billy was someone everyone shared. He even played rugby as well as Eddie could sing. Billy and Eddie had what you looked for in a great performer and once you saw it you never forgot it, because you didn't need it explaining to you. What Billy did came without explaining. It was clean and deep and so totally addictive you felt like a six year old hooked on Glenmorangie. There it was, the distant world in deepest Wigan, that smell of Africa on the wind in Ince Bar, or the kiss of a girl you'd met a million times in Oklahoma City in one of Eddie's slow songs. Billy came with it. You could take him anywhere. He was Wales and he was Africa, and when you saw him play he was everything you needed to make sense of the future. And later on, when Eddie got killed, Billy took over. He played lead guitar, without any fuss. He made things

move, while the Rugby Union crooned Perry Como.

We were integrated and didn't know it. Billy played with white South Africans like Fred Griffiths and Tommy Gentles and at other clubs Wilf Rosenberg and Len Killeen and Tom Van Vollenhoven regularly played against coloured opponents like Johnny Freeman. Wakefield, I remember, had a number of white South Africans like Coetzer, Prinsloo and Skene and many of the best clubs had players like Colin Dixon and Clive Sullivan. No one ever said this was strange, although at school it was strange because you weren't being taught it.

School was different. It taught you to be wholesome, for graded grains make finer flour. At the age of eleven boys were bleached white by the grammar-school system and those that weren't wandered away into the secondary moderns. In Wigan in the '50s grammar-school kids played Rugby Union while secondary moderns, the hewers of wood and drawers of water, played Rugby League. The association between sport and class was made explicit. To end up in a secondary modern, so you were told, was to enter a culture of mediocrity from which no one escaped. And that's what would have happened to a lot of lads but for Central Park. Central Park proved everything wrong. Wigan Rugby League Club was the place where the rejects came of age, those who had failed their eleven-plus exam and left school at fifteen and ended up in the same team as Fred Griffiths or Billy Boston. Here was a club run by ex-players, many of whom had gone the same route. Self-made and self-educated, the club directors had made good in construction and got a seat on the board. Men like Joe Taylor, who brought Billy Boston to Central Park, animated the life of

Wigan in the fifties and fired the aspirations of the youth of the town. Joe had the answers the grammar school hadn't. He knew exactly what we wanted and he told us not to be embarrassed by what others said of us in the 'kitchen-sink' books.

Football went one way, school another. The emotional loyalties generated by football and a school that encouraged you to bid your working-class loyalties a swift goodbye, made little sense. If school was a decision made for you, football was the community acting in spite of it. Football rejected the need to leave home, the school idea of 'onward and upward'. It created not a world unto itself, but a world beyond itself—the world outside —in its own backyard.

In some ways, Rugby League didn't spread because it didn't know how to. It stayed home and made the best of a bad job. And when anyone did leave or had to leave it was never easy to explain why, for the world outside seemed pale and unreal in comparison and people told you things about your community after a five-minute reading of George Orwell (an experience that moved them deeply, so they said) that made little sense. What you heard from others, as Joan Didion puts it, was 'the sermon in the suicide', the acquired narrative on working-class life that allowed those who had never set foot in the town to impose their own easy definition on the 'disparate images' you had left behind.[48] And to those who sniggered about the narrowness of the game, its provincial dullness and proletarian brutality, there was always the vital memory of colour—Roy Francis and George Bennett and, of course, Billy B.

Whatever its limitations Rugby League set its stall out to undermine the often stodgy respectability of Rugby Union. A willingness to take risks with the rules and a love of creative disobedience reminds us of the hipster's attitude towards conformity in Norman Mailer's essay 'The White Negro'. In the 1950s Mailer defined the enemy as a creeping totalitarianism, 'a slow death by conformity' which had resulted in 'every creative and rebellious instinct stifled'.[49] Mailer located his opposition to conformity in the figure of the hipster, a youthful risk-taker who struggled to uphold a kind of solitary courage; a spirit of adventure and dissent. It is this youthful fascination with the shock of the new that finds its embodiment in Rugby League, a game which has lead the way in innovation and progress over the best part of the twentieth century.[50]

In recent years Rugby Union has been forced to raise its standards in order to cope with the challenge mounted by Rugby League. The changes in law relating to scrummaging and kicking, the use of tactical substitutions, videos, physios, reserve team competitions, the increased number of points for a try, the use of sand, tees and commercial strips, not to mention the paying of players, all these are examples of the way the Rugby Football Union has modified its principles and unashamedly plagiarised the Rugby League game.

Clive Griffiths, fullback for Llanelli and Wales at Rugby Union and now one of the finest young coaches in British Rugby League, makes the following observation: 'There is no doubt in my mind', he says, 'that Rugby Union has analysed the professional Rugby League game and copied many if not all of its recent innovations'. The Rugby Union, Griffiths argues, has also been forced to change its attitude in order to keep pace with rising standards of fitness and athleticism. Indeed, some Rugby Union coaches have been quite happy to adopt the skills and conditioning technique of Rugby League teams. Griffiths refers us to the experience of Bath's Tom Hudson during the time he spent at Hull K.R. as well as Bob Dwyer's education in the Kangaroo training camp prior to the 1989 Rugby Union World Cup.[51] According to one writer in *The Financial Times*, 'It is fashionable for Rugby Union officials … to belittle Rugby League. This attitude is misplaced because, if anything, Union has copied far more from League these past years than vice versa'. Even the terminology has been copied. While 'it is commonplace to hear talk of a big hit, meaning a fierce tackle', it is distinctly uncommon to hear the commentator acknowledge—as in ITV's coverage of the Rugby Union World Cup—that 'these big hits have come from Rugby League and are a direct result of the extra emphasis now being placed on upper-body strength'.[52] According to Clive Griffiths, Rugby League terminology such as 'angles of running', 'control of the ball', 'kicking game', etc., is now an established part of the vocabulary of Rugby Union commentary, as are the statistics that came originally from American football into Australian Rugby League. Yet in spite of this, says Griffiths, 'and after listening to top Rugby Union players and being involved with and invited to the training sessions of many top Rugby Union clubs, Rugby League is still well ahead of Rugby Union in terms of tactics, innovation and level of analysis. Rugby Union players, he argues, 'still find it difficult to adapt to Rugby League'. Many of those who have reached the highest possible level in Rugby Union 'do not realise how intense and complicated the different defensive patterns are. There are also the technical and physical problems to cope with, such as the collision nature of the sport. Add to that the variations and tactics in attack such as the kick and chase game, and one can well understand why these players feel intimidated by the tasks they are asked to perform and the expectations placed upon them.

Griffiths describes the role of the prop forward to explain more specifically the difference between the codes:

In Rugby League the average prop will run with the ball approximately twenty, twenty five times a game and get tackled—often very early. He will then be expected to off load the ball in the tackle (which is an advanced handling skill) or catch and pass in one movement. Once his team have lost the ball he has then to defend. It is normal in a game for such a player to cover between 5,000 and 7,500 metres at varying speeds, moving forwards and backwards. He must be able to perform skills at maximum speed and withstand the rigour of hard bodily contact. Around the ruck or in general play he can make up to 30 tackles (sometimes more). In 80 minutes of play he is involved in 50 physical confrontations. Tack on the odd scrum and the funny business that goes with it and you can easily see how tough a position it is. Finally, there is the running off the ball in support or covering in defence. The player cannot stay on the ground.

In Rugby Union the scrummaging is far more technical and there is great physical pressure placed on the prop forward. But it is quite conceivable that a prop could go 80 minutes without handling the ball. He may rip a ball out of a maul or catch a kick but he will only drive into rucks and mauls, block at a lineout or lift the jumpers, scrummage 30 times and run from one set piece to another. He is hardly ever tackled. As far as physical conditioning is concerned the Rugby League prop is far more mobile and powerful—you only have to compare international players from both codes such as Chilcott and Platt.[53]

Phil Larder, national director of coaching in Rugby League over many years, offers other comparisons. He refers to a study undertaken in 1989 between two international stand-offs, Shaun Edwards (Rugby League) and Rob Andrew (Rugby Union). Each player's performance was broken down statistically in order to evaluate the extent of their involvement. The games that were chosen were test matches and both were played in 1989: Great Britain v New Zealand (Edwards) and Australia v British Lions (Andrew). Here is a table outlining the results.

A. Team Comparison

1. **Ball in Play**
Rugby League:
2nd Test Great Britain v New Zealand
51 minutes 17 seconds

Rugby Union:
2nd Test Australia v British Lions
21 minutes 52 seconds

2. **Total Involvement**
Rugby League:
2nd Test Great Britain v New Zealand

Tackles	221		
Passes	193		
Drives	158		
Kicks	24	Total Involvement	596

Rugby Union:
2nd Test Australia v British Lions

Tackles	62		
Passes	43		
Drives	57		
Kicks	38	Total Involvement	200

B. Player Comparison
1. **Tackles**
S. Edwards	13
R. Andrew	7

2. **Passes**
S. Edwards	43
R. Andrew	14

3. **Drives**
S. Edwards	9
R. Andrew	1

4. **Kicks**
S. Edwards	9
R. Andrew	13

Total Involvement
S. Edwards	79
R. Andrew	35

Physical Involvement
S. Edwards	13 + 14 : 27
R. Andrew	7 + 1 : 8

Some of the Comparisons
1. The ball was actually in play for two and a half times longer in the League game.
2. The total involvement of the teams was three times higher in the League game.
3. Shaun Edwards almost made twice as many tackles as Rob Andrew. It should, however, be pointed out that Andrew with 7 was the top tackler for the British Lions. Paul Hulme with 34, topped Great Britain's total.
4. Edwards' total involvement was twice as much as Andrew's, and he was involved in three times as many physical confrontations. [54]

According to Larder and Griffiths, both of whom have had long careers in Union and League, the Rugby Union player will find his code much easier to play and will be a better and more confident player—physically and mentally—should he decide to spend a period of time in Rugby League. [55]

Yet Rugby Union is still unable to acknowledge the influence Rugby League has had on it. Denial assumes a variety of forms. Des Seabrook, coach at Orrell, is alleged to have described Rugby League as a 'simple game for simple minds', a remark which, if true, indicts both his own environment as much as the Rugby League game which flourishes in it. Then there is the bile of the old boys to consider, those who stand at the apex of the pyramid of anti-northern prejudice. In 1990, Rod Rees, publicity officer at Neath, argued that Rugby League should not be 'allowed to use the word rugby', after a number of his players signed professionally. For Rees, 'All it has in common with Union is that it uses a ball of the same shape. Even that, so I am told, is lighter in weight which probably makes goal-kicking easier... As for scrummaging, I really don't know why they bother. It looks about as much like a scrum as I, in my 50s, look like an athlete'.[56] Equally common are the reactions of established or venerable players who use their role as journalists to rubbish the game. In one edition of *Rugby World* Vivian Jenkins describes Rugby League as 'abysmally boring to watch' a game where the players, as he puts it, refuse to 'run' and 'evade' each other. This comment was made in 1981 in an article on Fulham R.L.F.C. at a time when Fulham were attracting over 12,000 spectators to Craven Cottage. In 1981 Fulham were anything but boring. Featherstone perhaps. Bradford definitely. Warrington undeniably. But Fulham? In spite of overwhelming evidence to the contrary Jenkins trots out the hoary, old maxims. Rugby Union, he says, is professionally amateur and the reason the 'famous old ... clubs' in the North of England 'manage to survive' is because of their amateur ethos and their selfless camaraderie. (Virtues which are conspicuous by their absence in the money-grabbing world of Rugby League.)[57]

The trashing of Rugby League is a predictable occurrence in the national newspapers. Stephen Jones of *The Sunday Times* describes Rugby League as 'gaudy basketball', a game bereft of tension and intellectual resonance.[58] This claim is supported by Mick Cleary in *The Observer,* a regular jeremiad when it comes to commenting on Rugby League. Cleary utterly refutes the idea that Rugby League is quicker or more action-packed than Union. The argument is irrelevant, argues Cleary; 'sevens', he says, is more frantic than either but this does not make it a better game. As for Rugby League, it lacks depth and dimension to its patterns of play— the balance of the scrummage, the grace of the line out, the positional play of the ruck and maul. These skills and talents are frustrated in Rugby League, a game which denies the player the opportunity to express himself in complex and abstract ways.

Cleary is one of those pivotal figures who will go to any lengths in order to uphold the idea of the Rugby Union forward as a modern day athlete. He discusses the case of Stuart Evans, a Welsh Rugby Union prop who went from Neath to St. Helens in the late 1980s. Because he was a big man in Union, says Cleary, Evans should not be described as overweight or unfit or lacking the ball-handling skills. Nor is it useful to describe him as slow or unsupple or unaware of the essential tackling techniques that are taken for granted by Rugby League schoolboys. Evans, says Cleary, was none of those things that so shocked and traumatised the St. Helens' public when he first trundled out onto the Knowsley Road pitch. The Rugby League public, says Cleary, saw what it wanted to see. Skill is relative. The games are not comparable. Genius exists in the eyes of the beholder, etc., etc. Evans, says Cleary, was wasted in Rugby League because the directors, coaches and spectators at St. Helens could not distinguish between those who are 'fat' (a Rugby League word) and those who simply 'weigh more' than others (a Rugby Union expression). In other words, one man's 'fat' is another man's bulk. Rugby Union props are obliged to be 'bulky', says Cleary, in order to demonstrate the skills of the scrummage. The Rugby Union prop must 'block at a line-out' and ruck and maul, while a League prop is merely obliged to 'run, tackle and thrash about like a mating octopus at what passes for a scrummage'. Rugby Union, in other words, has no need to change its laws to quicken the game. 'To tamper with the laws in any sport for the benefit of the spectator is a dangerous business'. Who wants to see Artie Beetson or Andy Platt when you can see Stuart Evans or Jeff Probyn? To change the laws, says Cleary, is to reduce Rugby Union to 'a much simpler version' of a complex art form, merely for the sake of 'lots of running, lots of tackles, and lots of tries'. This is to create rugby on tap, fast-food rugby, the sporting equivalent of the convenience store. Rugby League has already done this, says Cleary. Which is why the game lacks finesse and pattern. Rugby League is rugby made easy; rugby designed for the secondary moderns. It fakes the action and omits the strategy—the intellectual definition which precedes the action. As a puzzle it is without difficulty, the need to unravel a pattern of play before the act of high-definition performance can begin. As a contest it never goes beyond an act of collision and random gyration in order to work itself out in theatrical form. Rugby League is pure sex but no more. It gets to the action without the courtship. It is puréed page three from beginning to end.[59]

In the quality press definitions belong to Rugby Union definers. Whatever its achievements on the field, Rugby League struggles to make itself heard above the din that is generated by those in the media who represent the interests of fifteen-a-side. Once we leave the field of play we struggle to find an articulate presentation, a cogent voice that can give the game a sense of direction. Those who speak out for Rugby League in a clear and articulate voice, like Paul Fitzpatrick in *The Guardian* or Dave Hadfield in *The Independent,* find themselves opposed by a huge army of establishment court historians,

each of whom is allowed a seemingly endless number of column inches per article in order to report the most trivial of Rugby Union events. A lot of that reporting takes the form of aggressive propaganda. And whatever the resilience of Rugby League, the game is not invulnerable to attack. Sooner or later the armour is pierced, the barb draws blood and the hipster is wounded. The Rugby Union war of attrition is highly effective. It is a long-haul strategy designed to undermine the self-worth of its opponent. It relies on the cumulative impact of years of casual, careless discourtesy cultural condescension for the provincial north in a thousand ways.

We find it hard to fight back. We are 'white negroes' only on the field of play. Harry Sunderland apart, we have no tradition after 1895 of active subversion, no 'Black Jacobins', no Toussaint L'Ouverture's who rescue the game with revolutionary thought. When it comes to the art of political resistance Rugby League is conservative and the 'white negro' style has not been marketed the way it should have been. The Rugby Union has spoilt things. To them we are no more than a bunch of 'white niggers', a yard gang who have deliberately chosen to evict themselves from the sporting community, and cannot decide, like William Faulkner's Joe Christmas, whether they'd rather be white or black. They accuse us of being incomplete, of lacking a name and lacking a nature. This is the reason we are watched so intently; as if—in the words of Faulkner's Eupheus Hines—our presence is a 'sign' of 'God's abomination'.[60]

The accusation of incompleteness has left an indelible mark on the character of Rugby League. It wounds us and in some way we play the game in order to disguise that wound. Off the field the wound re-opens and festers easily. For a hundred years we have been described as prodigal and delinquent. We are weary of the charge yet the parent is relentless and still disowns us. However much we conspire to agree never to be like him we cannot choose to be indifferent to his remarks. For him we remain the psychopathic child, the wanton orphan, the fugitive infant on the run from history. The loss of a protective and advising parent never allows us to be embraced or forgiven. We find we have entered an absurd universe in which the world prefers the abuse of the parent to the defiance of the child. We are, therefore, not sufficiently, listened to. The recognition we seek, that place in the sun the Rugby Union has long denied us—the dream of becoming a national sport—can never be ours.

There are other problems. Rugby League clubs, whatever their socialist traditions, are highly commercial organisations. They have boards of directors who must generate capital, create and invest in new resources and balance the books at the shareholders' meeting at the end of the year. They are obliged to sell a product—the game itself—to an increasingly discerning sporting public. This becomes difficult when their credibility is undermined by those who publicise—as the Rugby Union do—the disobedience and treachery of 1895. How can the clubs reasonably satisfy their sponsors if the public is told over and over that the game lacks discipline and a sense of authority?

Throughout its history Rugby League has been at pains to disprove these accusations and to demonstrate its managerial skills. A game that is riddled with anarchy and lawlessness can hardly be run as a sound business venture, nor can it inspire the confidence of the shareholders. The task has not been an easy one.

As Dai Davies shows us, the problem of authority has bedeviled Rugby League and has been one of the most complex and unlovely features of our game since the 1920s. Pomposity and extravagant self-regard have characterised many of our officials and directors, as if they have become overwhelmed by the need to prove how tough they are in order to eliminate the memory of disobedience —the historical sin of 1895.

How else can one possibly explain the damage inflicted on the game over the last few years as a result of the feud between the Rugby Football League in Leeds and the British Amateur Rugby League Association in Huddersfield over the question of which body was responsible for the organisation of youth rugby? The conflict began when the Rugby League decided to establish youth teams at professional clubs—what they called Academy sides. By establishing an Academy competition Rugby League clubs were able to create feeder sides for the professional clubs, thereby depriving the amateur leagues of their most gifted players at youth and Under 19's level. In retaliation, B.A.R.L.A. insisted that any player who signed as an amateur for a professional club had profess-ionalised himself and forfeited his amateur status. The Rugby League replied by banning amateur clubs from the Regal Trophy and Challenge Cup and by denying B.A.R.L.A. the use of all Rugby League facilities. From 1990-1993 leading officials on both sides played out a game of power politics in an attempt to discredit each others position. The impact on the game's public image was disastrous. The warring factions conducted their dispute in the national media with the dominant personalities of the rival adminis-trations pursuing what Bob Ashby, Chairman of the Rugby League, described as 'a struggle to the death'.

In this 'struggle' each side felt compelled to play the father-figure card. The Rugby

League assumed the role of authoritarian, wilfully plagiarising the attitude, if not the position, of the Rugby Union. The attempt to disinvent B.A.R.L.A. gave the impression that the Rugby League was seeking to fill the vacuum created by 1895; to resolve, in other words, the problem of lost parenthood. Having found itself in the company of a wayward child, the Rugby League decided to adopt the persona of the father it had once denied—the very father it had walked out on in 1895. It even admitted, as Dave Hadfield suggests in *Open Rugby*, 'that the object of [the] whole exercise [had] been to grind [B.A.R.L.A.] into the dirt'. B.A.R.L.A., on the other hand, refused to accept its punishment and seemed to believe that it did not come from a legitimate source. From its reading of history B.A.R.L.A. realised that in a war of father against father, the sensitivity of the Rugby Football League on the issue of parenthood could be easily exploited. Better for B.A.R.L.A. to throw in its lot with the Rugby Union in a grand alliance of grandson and grandad. Thus B.A.R.L.A. reacted to the threat of punishment by asking for help from the original father, the authentic father, the absent ancestor. A cap-in-hand meeting was arranged between the Secretary of the Rugby Football Union, Dudley Wood (the biggest big daddy of them all), and officials from B.A.R.L.A. in which Wood was asked to write a letter on behalf of B.A.R.L.A. which could then be circulated to those amateur bodies claiming an affiliation with the Rugby League. Such a letter was sent to B.A.R.L.A. from Dudley Wood at Twickenham on 6 November 1992 and was subsequently circulated to each of the offending amateur bodies on 18 November. In this letter of 18 November B.A.R.L.A. issued a general warning (backed up with the letter of support from Wood) indicating that any amateur association that retained a link—however tenuous—with the Rugby Football League was guilty of professionalising itself. This act, says Dave Hadfield, was 'reminiscent of the blackballing strategy of Rugby Union that [B.A.R.L.A.] used to complain about so loudly'. It represented 'an unforgivable' betrayal of history.

Many of the actions of Rugby League officials betray a lack of genuine confidence in their own status. While many of these officials think of themselves as a definitive voice of northern culture, their dreams are troubled by the sins which others have attributed to them. Hence the need to act tough. Demonstrations of toughness represent a recurrent rather than a recent phenomena in the history of the game. Beneath that toughness lies an insecurity. And because of it, we must keep what happened in 1895 in some kind of perspective.

1895 drew a large line across history but, almost immediately, the act of secession began to trouble certain of our officials, as did the numerous social divisions which the game found itself unable to break down. If Rugby League had placed itself on the right side of history, there were always those who remained deeply suspicious of the unruly forces the game had unleashed. A tension soon arose between those who saw the need to purge Rugby League of its individualism and unbridled class ambition and those who saw the game in a more democratic light, as a forum for expressing the hopes and dreams of the working class. This tension has persisted throughout much of the twentieth century and it was something Dai Davies was forced to encounter throughout his career. [61]

When Dai accepted the offer of Broughton Rangers in 1925 he joined a club with a rich Rugby League tradition. Broughton, however, had fallen on hard times and

121

seemed to be regressing into a state of authoritarianism, a Victorian mindset from which, in the 1890s, it had tried so hard to escape. Instead of modernising itself and adapting its policies to the needs of the 1920s Broughton had become obsessed with preserving its status as a founder club. For Dai Davies, the visible symbols of hierarchy, heroism and self-regard were the wax moustaches of the club directors and their finger-wagging, regimental manner. The bullying approach of men like Major Hampson did little to raise morale at Broughton and was one of the reasons why Dai eventually left the club. Dai hated the penny-pinching, on-the-cheap attitude of Broughton and the cynical way it exploited players like him, who travelled north with little knowledge of Rugby League and none whatsoever of contractual relationships.

Broughton left its mark on Dai. Lack of loyalty at the top and the realisation that the committee man might always be willing to place his own needs above those of his players made Dai suspicious of those in positions of authority. Even at Warrington, a club which treated him like the Crown Jewels, Dai never found it that easy to walk away from controversy or to ignore the actions of those whom he felt had failed to represent his interests properly. To be fair, this was an uncommon experience for Dai at Warrington and the club had a genuine sense of welfare for its players. But because of his past experience Dai tended to retain his suspicion of those whose motives he regarded as vicarious or self-serving. He was uncompromising in his opposition to men of political ambition and his frequent clashes with Canon Bardsley, the Tory Councillor, may well have hastened his departure from the club. In moments of crisis Dai tended to see himself in the role of the persecuted outsider, as the picaresque Jew, Lazarillo de Tormes, who lives off his wits to stay out of trouble. That sometimes Dai didn't learn quick enough or move fast enough was something he found difficult to accept, especially when it resulted in his failure to secure a tour place to Australia in 1932. In Dai's opinion, the man who was responsible for this betrayal was the tour manager, Bob Anderton, a man whom many of the Warrington players regarded as a father-figure. In Dai's opinion, Anderton had deliberately refused to nominate him for a place on the tour. This provided him with yet another example of official disloyalty.

We will never know whether or not Dai was correct to harbour these suspicions about Anderton. It would certainly be wrong to deny that some of Dai's problems were of his own making. Beneath the outrageous self-confidence there lay a nagging insecurity, a constant need to be told how good he was and how much he was loved. As a man preoccupied with moral opinion Dai took a firm and frequent stand on matters of principle when, perhaps, the more prudent approach would have been to bide his time and say nothing. (This was the case at Thames Board Mills when he lost his job in an argument over a pittance.) At Broughton, he regarded a cut in wages as an insult to his talent, and for this reason returned home. It was not in his nature to play bottom-dog or to be pushed around by men whose stuffy elitism and watch-chain manner he had no time for. If Dai was the target-man of the team, the most talented player in the club, he was also its most celebrated rebel. It was Dai that spoke up for Jack Elwyn Evans and Evan Phillips when the call came through to the chemist's shop in Garnant. Dai relished the opportunity. Directors like Kennedy meant nothing to him. They did not even begin to measure up to the standards set by his parents in

Garnant and the love and loyalty his father had shown him in the anthracite mines.

After he left Broughton Dai always claimed he trusted no one. When the directors at Wigan tried to sign him and told him to take the advice of Jim Sullivan, Dai was contemptuous: 'No Jim was going to put me right', he used to say. 'I was going to put myself right'. Dai deliberately overdid the braggadocio, although typically he would never admit it. Certain people, of course, he always trusted —his mates at Warrington like Candy Evans and Jess Meredith, Bill Shankland and Jackie Oster and, above all, Jack Hamblet, his friend in the boot room for over fifty years. Dai was good with the bluff and he prided himself on the quickness of his wit. His defiance at the time Wigan tried to sign him speaks volumes for the pain he experienced at the break-up of his family, many of whom were invaluable as a source of guidance and counselling. By the time Dai signed for Warrington there was nothing his family could do for him, and nothing, more importantly, that he could do any longer for the family. His father had split the home up; Will, his brother, was in America; his sister was in Ammanford; and his mother, like his older brother Tom, was already dead. This was a big blow to Dai. He felt at the time he could never trust anyone the way he had trusted his own family. It would take a good few years of marriage before he could begin to see things differently.

Dai's wife, Katie, was instrumental in bringing about a change of attitude. She worked wonders, one suspects, especially in times of emotional difficulty, in keeping Dai on an even keel. She faced, moreover, an uphill task. The loss of an entire family must have devastated Dai. I often wonder about the impact such a loss must have had on Dai's personality, and whether his moments of volatility can best be explained as the actions of a man wrestling with the pain and guilt of what he had left behind him in Wales. Others have argued that Dai courted confrontation and that he was only happy when picking a fight, as if driven by the need to purge himself of the sin he had committed in abandoning his family.

The charge of recklessness does not hold up. Dai was a naturally spirited character but his abrasive manner did not originate in some deranged guilt, nor was it induced by the loneliness of life in the north of England. Wherever he was—at school, colliery, rugby club—and whatever the company, Dai was full of tricks. On the other hand, he was a rugby player of immense seriousness who worked hard at his game in order to improve it. He was sent off only once in his career and was not known for being malicious or vindictive. Dai fought his corner and his strong belief in natural justice brought him into regular conflict with authority. But he always devoted himself to being a craftsman. He watched others who were craftsmen and was never too proud to learn new skills. During the inter-war period he was one of the finest scrum halves in the game, an artist rather than a rough house, a ball distributor with an incomparable ability to create an opening out of nothing. If Dai had a weak point it was his tackling, for his style of play was not like that of an extra loose forward— such as David Hulme or David Bishop. Instead, he was a player who could scheme his way in and out of a game almost at will. His forté was to break from the scrum on the blind side, draw the loose forward and the fullback, then switch the ball back inside. Bill Shankland, the Australian centre who played for Warrington in the 1920s and '30s and who subsequently became the British Ryder Cup golf coach, once said of Dai that he was a generation ahead of his time and possessed an extraordinary ability to change his game in order to adapt to the skills of his opponent.[62] In everything he did, says Shankland, Dai was creative.

Dai's career transcended the numerous little local difficulties which came his way and he ought to be remembered for his sense of hope, a spiritual exuberance that allowed him to overcome the personal setbacks and career disappointments that would have crushed and demoralised a lesser person. Dai did not run away or retreat into a shell at the first sign of difficulty, which has been the case with some Union players who have not made the grade. Although bitterly disappointed at the hand fate dealt him, from time to time, he never forgot how to make the best of things. My abiding memory of Dai is seeing him in the Garnant club, like some ancient imp with springs on his bottom, bobbing up and down as he told a story; or at home, with that toothless grin of his, as he started to recall a favourite joke about Albert Harding. Dai was a man of character and a man of style and he left an indelible impression on those who watched him and played alongside him. In checking the reports of his performances in the *Evening Post, Amman Valley Chronicle, Athletic News, Daily Dispatch, Salford City Reporter*, the overwhelming impression is of an incisive and gifted player who always refused to play second fiddle, whatever the opposition—Bob Delahey, W.C. Powell, 'Chimpy' Busch, Jonathan Parkin. As John Burn puts it: 'He played in the first Rugby League match I ever saw in November 1926 when I was eleven years old. Even after all these years in my mind's eye I still see him and admire his brilliant play for Broughton Rangers. In the ensuing sixty years I have seen all the great players, and he, for my money, remains one of the very best'.[63] Jack Hamblet, who worked at Warrington for fifty years, claims, in his letters, that Dai was the finest half back to play for the club and he includes players of international renown like the great Australian, Bobby Fulton. Fifty years after he left Warrington Dai is still fondly remembered. In a letter to Bill Davies, Dai's son, Ernie Day refers to 'the many thousands of players to whom Dai gave pleasure in his own inimitable way'.[64]

Dai earned respect. In my research I have encountered little to suggest that the Amman community was anything other than unreservedly proud of his achievements. This may have something to do with the closely-knit village traditions, the communal structures and cultural politics of a mining people. Certainly, the absence of envy is remarkable, given what others have had to put up with. Dai's signing was even greeted in the press as an honour for the community. The week before he went north a huge farewell concert was thrown in The Half Moon Hotel. The local newspaper, the *Amman Valley Chronicle*, records the event with gusto:

> The space required to accommodate the huge numbers of friends to both players who had attended to extend their best wishes on their departure was quite inadequate and quite a number were obliged to enter into the convivialities from the landing outside. The event was without doubt of high order, was quite orderly and edifying throughout. The proceedings were conducted under the presidency of Mr. F.W. Gunning and a number of good singers contributed towards a classical and appropriate programme. Mr. Gunning at the outset delivered a suitable address, and Mr. Giraldus Rees opened the musical items with an overture on the piano. The following contributed items to the programme:—Messrs. Emrys Davies, Percy Rees, George Evans, Emrys Pritchard, Dan Davies, Wm. Benjamin, D.M. Davies,

Gomer Griffiths and Mesach Phillips. Verses composed for the occasion by Mr. Richard Evans were read and gave cause for much laughter. Messrs. Giraldus Rees and David J. Rees were the able accompanists. The most important function of the evening was the presentation of a cheque to each of the players honoured, contributed solely by their numerous friends. This pleasant duty was admirably performed by Mr. Tom Evans, the popular Amman and Neath forward, who made an inspiring speech in handing over the cheques with the best wishes of the donors. The recipients suitably responded.

On his own admission Dai was known as an 'awkward little bugger', a man of mischief and cheek. (The *Amman Valley Chronicle* uses the word 'vivacious'.[65]) But the people loved him for it. Alan Leigh, the curator of Warrington Museum, tells how Dai had a reputation for playing games with the town's bus drivers. He would wait at a bus stop and as the bus slowed down to pick him up he would turn his back and wander off. As the bus picked up speed Dai would count to five and give chase. He used to reckon that if he caught the bus and jumped on board within twenty-five yards his fitness was in order.

Like Alex Murphy and Andy Gregory, Dai Davies had Rugby League written all over him. He was totally and utterly suited to the game. A player with supreme confidence in his ability on the field, he was not averse to the odd bit of praise once he was off it. Dai was not a man who was backward in coming forward. The first time I met him in the Garnant club he was still giving jip. Seventy-six years old and Dai was full of it, as he caught the rising wave with his chatter. Right to the end, like Billy B. in the early years, he surfed the hurricane.

NOTES

[1] Robert Hughes, *Culture of Complaint: the Fraying of America* (New York: Oxford University Press, 1993).

[2] Geoffrey Moorhouse, *At The George and other Essays on Rugby League,* (London: Hodder & Stoughton, 1989), 136.

[3] Ibid., 135, 42. An example of the quiet dignity of Rugby League would be the way it has chosen to commemorate the dead. Fred Holcroft refers to the high number of soldiers from the Wigan area who fought in the Lancashire Fusiliers and Royal Lancasters and were killed during the Boer War at the Battle of Spion Kop. The famous hill at Wigan's Central Park is named Spion Kop in memory of those who lost their lives. Fred Holcroft, *The Devil's Hill: Local Men at the Battle of Spion Kop, 1900* (Wigan Heritage Service Publications: 3, 1992).

[4] Moorhouse, op.cit., 73.

[5] Martine Kettle, 'It's just not Cricket', *The Guardian,* 22 June 1993, 10-11.

[6] Moorhouse, op.cit., 30.

[7] Moorhouse, op.cit., 67.

[8] Chris Rea, 'All Blacks meet the Kiwi Challenge', *The Independent On Sunday,* 20 June 1993, 29.

[9] Harry Edgar, 'Good Luck Terry Holmes', *Open Rugby,* number 81, January 1986, 5.

[10] Nick Garnett, 'The Closed Minds of Open Rugby', *Financial Times,* 31 August 1985, Section II.

[11] Nick Garnett, 'Trying to Break Free', *Financial Times,* 29 April/30 April 1989, Section II.

[12] Dudley Wood, Letter to *The Times,* 13 May 1993.

[13] Robert Armstrong, 'A man inspired by pride and faith', *The Guardian,* 28 June 1993.

[14] Toni Morrison, *Beloved,* (New York: Knopf, 1987), 190.

[15] Barbara Christian, '*From the Inside Out: Afro-American Women Literary Tradition and the State*', (Center for Humanitistic Studies Occasional Papers, University of Minnesota Press, 1986).

[16] Moorhouse, op.cit., 85.

[17] Morrison, op.cit., 125.

[18] Quoted in G. D. Killam (ed), *African Writers on African Writing,* (London: Heinemann, 1973), 7.

[19] Sandra Cisneros: 'From the Barrio to the Brownstone', *Los Angeles Times,* 7 May 1991, Section F1, F7.

[20] Maxine Hong Kingston, *The Woman Warrior,* (London: Picador), Pan Books, 1981), 149-50.

[21] David Irvine, 'Heslop hits Orrell by moving to League', *The Guardian,* 17 February 1993, 16.

[22] John Kennedy, 'Now RL goes after star boys', *Western Mail,* 26 October 1990, 30. See also Martin Pitchwell, 'League out to get Us!' *Herald of Wales,* 27 April 1989, 48.

[23] Quoted in letter from Jack McNamara, 14 January 1993. McNamara cites his source as *The Sunday Telegraph,* December 1985.

[24] Garnett, 'Trying to break Free', op.cit.

[25] Martin Pitchwell, 'TARGET! They're gunning for Jonathan', Swansea *Herald of Wales,* 12 January 1989, 40.

[26] Quoted in letter from Jack McNamara, 14 January 1993. McNamara cites his source as *The Times,* 23 December 1985.

[27] In 1982 after watching the Australian Kangaroos in the second test at Wigan, Thomas said: 'There can be little doubt that these great Australians are one of the greatest rugby teams ever to visit our shores. They would rank with the 1951 Sprinboks, 1967 All Blacks and 1971 Lions in New Zealand. Their professionalism is such that, with two extra men, they would convincingly beat any of the four home countries at the Rugby Union game'. Clem Thomas, 'No holding these kangaroos down', *The Observer,* 21 November 1982, 41. In 1986 Thomas wrote that: 'After nearly 40 years in the opposite camp, I now believe Rugby League is a better game to watch and play than Rugby Union. In stating my heresy, I have met surprisingly few arguments from my Union friends; indeed the majority agree with me'. Clem Thomas, 'Why I have joined the League of gentlemen', *The Observer,* 30 November 1986, 50.

[28] 'Guardians of Rugby', *Evening Post,* 25 February 1976.

[29] Barrie Fairall, 'Ireland's double bonus', *The Guardian,* 19 January 1984, 25.

[30] For a report on the scandal of tax-free payments in Rugby Union see Jeremy Alexander and Neil Robinson, 'Pilgrim's progress may lead RFU to valley of humiliation', *The Guardian,* 21 August 1993. It's also worth noting that during the Whitbread Rugby World Awards televised on 11 May 1993, Chris Rea told the audience how David Campese had become a millionaire from playing Rugby Union in Italy. The audience laughed with knowing approval. The astonishing lengths to which Union commentators will go in order to deny the existence of shamateurism in Rugby Union is again illustrated by Rea in *The Observer,* 'I have yet to meet any player, committed to remaining in Rugby Union, who believes that he should be paid for playing'. Chris Rea, 'Union dues to be paid', *The Observer,* 19 November 1989, 32.

[31] Moorhouse, op.cit., 4.

[32] Quoted in Wilfred Stone, *The Cave and the Mountain,* (Stanford, California: Stanford University Press; London: University Press, 1966), 250.

[33] Martin J. Wiener, *English Culture and the Decline of the Industrial Spirit, 1850-1980,* (Cambridge: Cambridge University Press, 1984), 20.

[34] Wiener, op.cit., 41-2.

[35] Moorhouse, op.cit., 39.

[36] John Hopkins, 'Why Wembley lacks Twickenham's rugby soul', *The Observer,* October 1992.

[37] Garnett, op.cit., 'The closed minds of open rugby'.

[38] 'Paradise Re-Visited', *Open Rugby,* number 81, January 1986, 16.

[39] Moorhouse, op.cit., 80.

[40] 'Rugby club "forgets" its famous RL coach', *Yorkshire Post,* 21 September 1978.

[41] McNamara, op.cit.

[42] Moorhouse, op.cit., 74-5, 6.

[43] Robert Fassolette, 'Looking for the light', *Open Rugby,* number 134, April 1991, 38.

[44] 'The Scandal', *Open Rugby,* number 118, October 1989, 14.

[45] Joe Ashton, 'Game of two halves', *The Guardian,* 30 October 1992, 21; Matthew Engel, 'Sack, "arrogant" old guard or else—ANC', *The Guardian,* 13 November 1992, 21.

[46] Ian Malin, 'WRU forced to break silence on fees for S.A. tour', *The Guardian,* 5 February, 1993, 19.

[47] Colin Price, 'Out of the Wood!' *Daily Mirror,* 5 August 1993, 39; Mike Averis, 'Wood's "black influence" denial fails to placate athletes', *The Guardian,* 6 August 1993, 19.

[48] Joan Didion's *The White Album,* (Harmondsworth: Penguin, 1981), 11.

[49] Norman Mailer, 'The White Negro', *Dissent,* IV (Summer 1957), 276-293. Reprinted in Gene Feldman and Max Gartenberg (eds), *The Beat Generation and the Angry Young Men,* (New York: Citadel Press, 1958), 342-363.

[50] Clem Thomas is one of the few eminent Rugby Union commentators to publicly acknowledge the various innovations. He suggests that: 'intelligent and

judicious law changes have developed a game which delights both the player and spectator'. League, he says, is 'a mile ahead of anything in Union'. 'Why I have joined the League of gentlemen', op.cit.

⁵¹ Clive Griffiths, letter to the author, 19 June 1993.

⁵² John Hopkins, 'Two codes, one language', *Financial Times Weekend,* 1/2 May 1993.

⁵³ Griffiths, op.cit.

⁵⁴ Phil Larder, 'League is Streets Ahead!' *Open Rugby,* number 124, April 1990, 34.

⁵⁵ Geoff Green makes the following bizarre observation: 'One of the nice things about Rugby Union is the way it offers something for just about every type of player. The short, fat prop who can't run too fast can still enjoy a game on a Saturday. He wouldn't be either fit enough or quick enough to play RL'. Geoff Green, 'Changing rules is not the way', *Manchester Evening Post,* 20 December 1986, 21.

⁵⁶ 'In Touch with Richard Thomas', *South Wales Evening Post,* 10 November 1990, 13.

⁵⁷ Vivian Jenkins, 'Fulham Succeed will London Fail?' *Rugby World,* January 1981, 11.

⁵⁸ Stephen Jones, 'Tinker, tinker—but it could have been worse', *The Sunday Times,* 23 September 1990, 18.

⁵⁹ Mick Cleary, 'Playing the PR game', *Observer,* 23 September 1990, 23.

⁶⁰ William Faulkner, *Light in August,* (New York: Random House, 1959), 284.

⁶¹ Dave Hadfield, 'War! What is it Good For?' *Open Rugby,* number 138, October 1991, 17.

⁶² Letter from Bill Shankland to the author, 21 October 1991.

⁶³ Letter from John Burn to the author, 12 March 1987.

⁶⁴ Letter from Ernie Day to the author, 10 January 1993.

⁶⁵ 'Farewell Concert', *Amman Valley Chronicle,* 11 February 1926; 'A Strong Friendship', *Amman Valley Chronicle,* 8 April 1926.

Index

130